THE BUSINESS OF SPECIAL EVENTS

Fundraising Strategies for Changing Times

Harry A. Freedman
and Karen Feldman

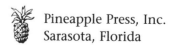 Pineapple Press, Inc.
Sarasota, Florida

Inquiries should be addressed to:
Pineapple Press, Inc.
P.O. Box 3899
Sarasota, Florida 34230

Library of Congress Cataloging in Publication Data

Freedman, Harry A.
     The business of special events / by Harry A. Freedman and
Karen Feldman. — 1st ed.
          p.   cm.
     ISBN 1-56164-141-3   (pbk. : alk. paper)
     1. Fund raising. 2. Promotion of special events. 3. Public
relations. I. Feldman, Karen.   II. Title.
HV41.2.F74   1997
658.15′224—dc21   97-28397
                                                              CIP

First Edition
10 9 8 7 6 5 4 3 2 1

Design by Carol Tornatore
Printed and bound by BookCrafters, Chelsea, Michigan

TABLE OF CONTENTS

Since our first book, *Black Tie Optional*, debuted seven years ago, we have traveled around the country teaching people how to increase their fundraising know-how. Many participants said that the book proved invaluable in planning and staging successful events.

But many things have changed in those seven years. Costs have risen and the number of fundraising groups has soared, making the competition for support much tougher. People kept asking us for an updated book that addressed the latest challenges in producing special events. This is our response to that need.

ACKNOWLEDGMENTS

Advance readers of *The Business of Special Events* frequently praised the book's businesslike approach to events. Realizing that charities are coming under ever more public scrutiny regarding how they use their money, several readers said this book helped them make more responsible decisions. Still others appreciated that the book provides tools to do this and information on incorporating new computer technology to make the job easier.

We were delighted that Pineapple Press publishers June and David Cussen saw the value of this book, too, and the importance of making it more widely available, since our mail-order-only *Black Tie Optional* was the sole reference source on the market for planning special events.

We owe thanks once again to Dick Stolley, senior editorial adviser for Time, Inc., for his wisdom, support, and always helpful advice.

Harry's sister, Susan Freedman, again came to our aid by attending to many of the details a book like this requires.

Harry's twenty-five years as a fundraiser and Karen's twenty as a journalist proved a great match. Our prepublication readers tell us the result of that collaboration is a book that is easy to use, packed with information, and that even produces a laugh now and then on a topic that often causes reactions less pleasant.

Our thanks go to Pineapple Press—for the staff's patience, understanding, editing, and support. We are especially indebted to Amanda Oswald, who shepherded this book and its authors through the rigors of the editing and publishing processes. And thanks to Gale Research's Taft subsidiary, which granted permission for another publisher to handle this latest effort.

And, of course, there are those personal acknowledgments:

From Harry:

A project like this would never have happened without the encouragement and support of colleagues and friends, including: Milton B. Suchin, Harvey Burstein, Susan Baker, Sandie Cauff, Gene Luntz, Greg DiStefano, Philip and Marilyn Langer, Celia Lipton Farris, and Gina Franano.

Special thanks go to Sherry and Ron Funt, Sue Weiss and Joe Cedillos, Miriam Brown, Ed Yoe, Roger Levin and Sally King, Bill Harris, Jake Wengroff, and Joe Farina, who were always there for me when things were not so special!

I am also very grateful for having had the privilege to learn from great talents such as Bob and Dolores Hope, Phyllis Diller, Dick Clark, Peter Max, Gloria and Emilio Estefan, Patti LaBelle, Tony Bennett, Debbie Reynolds, and many other gifted celebrities.

A special note of gratitude goes to my parents, Benjamin Feir and Irene Schaeffer Feir. They both encourage the many things I do both professionally and personally. I am especially grateful to them for their continued love and patience, especially during those times when I have said "yes" to far too many projects.

My son, Brian, a computer whiz and up-and-coming computer consultant, helps to remind me that there are still many things I need to take the time to learn, as well as taking time out to smell the roses. His concern and love for his dad do not go unnoticed and, in fact, he is a constant source of pride.

From Karen:

This revision wouldn't have been possible without the support and counsel of Nickie Haggart and Suzie Benton, women of great insight and caring who have helped keep life manageable.

Special thanks to Ed Clement and Roslyn Anderson, who endured and supported me through the entire process.

It is virtually impossible to adequately thank my parents, Jerry and Adele Feldman, who have given me unflagging love and support, not to mention a first-rate education.

Lastly, I am forever grateful to my four-legged roommates—Gwen, Rovic, Harry, Squeaky, Max, Moorestown, and Lily—who were always available for love and lap-sitting at the computer.

INTRODUCTION

In every community, special events take place almost daily. The swearing in of a government official, a church concert, a black-tie charity ball, a pancake breakfast, a beach bash, and many other happenings all qualify as special events. Some are held to raise money, some to build a constituency. No matter what the purpose, all require solid business planning to be successful.

Most of us get drafted to serve on a committee at some time in our lives. Some are lucky and wind up on a committee of a well-organized, established group that has records of previous events — names of vendors, possible sites, budgets, maybe even reports of what worked and what didn't.

For those faced with rounding up a new committee, it pays to make sure the committee reflects a cross section of the community — working people, social and professional leaders — representing a range of economic levels, ethnic groups, and areas of expertise.

The most important question a committee must answer is, "Should we even attempt a special event?" If not, what are the alternatives? Other questions include:

- What type of event should it be?
- What will it cost?
- How will you attract people and money to it?
- Where should you hold it?

This book will help you answer all these questions.

A special event must be run like a business. If it isn't, it is bound to lose money. However, unlike successful businesses, special events are often run by inexperienced people—frequently, these people are volunteers with good intentions but unrealistic expectations. No matter what type of event it is, there are basic ingredients required to make it successful. Chief among them are adequate human resources, good financial management, and a highly organized plan.

These are the same qualities that have raised money since recorded history began . . . and probably even before that. When Christopher Columbus wanted to sail in search of the Indies, his friends and family refused to help pay for what they thought was a far-fetched mission. But he convinced Spain's Queen Isabella, and in a fifteenth-century version of corporate underwriting, she agreed to pay for the expedition.

While Columbus used a direct appeal for support, many organizations have used special events to raise money. For centuries, charitable fundraising was an activity limited to the upper classes, who hosted elaborate balls, festivals, symphonies, and operas to fund their pet causes. With the advent of federal income taxes in the early 1900s and the subsequent write-offs created for charitable giving, the rich had more incentive than ever to contribute. But other than churches, there were few nonprofit organizations to which they could donate.

However, since World War II, the number of fundraising organizations has exploded. That number climbed from fewer than 1,000 in the late 1940s, to 200,000 in 1980 to almost 600,000 in 1995. Of the $150.7 billion donated to nonprofits in 1996, the American Association of Fundraising Counsel reports that 45.3% went to religious causes. Giving in general rose by more than 7% but corporate giving dropped to 4.7%, down from 5.1% in 1995. The vast majority of donations—80.9%—came from individuals.

Wealthy people used to do their charitable giving at lavish affairs for a select few. Today, a fundraiser can be a worldwide event, with countries linking up via satellite, the Internet, and the telephone. People of all ages, ethnicities, and socioeconomic conditions can participate in events like Comic Relief, which collects millions of dollars each year to feed the poor. The Olympics in Atlanta in the summer of 1996 were underwritten by fundraisers that took place in towns and cities around the world. Major events today are feeling the crunch of rising overhead. Like the Olympics, they need substantial corporate sponsorship or underwriting.

Never has the need for money been so great. Governments—national, state, and local—continue to chop away at funding they once provided to nonprofits, leaving a heavier burden for individuals and corporations. While private-sector giving may be on the rise, the portion that goes toward social service has not kept pace with rising demand and costs. Further, major businesses are merging or downsizing; corporations are slashing budgets, and thus are less able to give to causes they once supported. The consolidation of many companies also means there are fewer sources to tap and fewer employees at those that remain. It would not be surprising if traditional sources of funds for good causes disappear entirely in the near future.

Fundraisers all over the country say it is more and more difficult to attract enough money from the private sector to provide basic services as those services escalate in cost. Heading into the twenty-first century, the adage that charity begins at home has never been truer.

Fundraising consultant Lloyd B. Dennis told the Los Angeles Society of Fund Raising Executives in 1996, "This is a revolutionary time for nonprofits... a time when many may be swept away. Those that are creative and highly businesslike will survive. Those who are not, will not."

There's no magic to creating a great special event. Some very specific things have to happen at precisely the right times. Knowing how to accomplish that is the trick. Besides offering easy-to-understand techniques, this book provides checklists for quick reference and worksheets to help plan budgets, set ticket prices, organize committees, and publicize events. It gives planners information on how and where to look for sponsors and underwriting, how to attract big-name entertainment and book them for events, and still manage to make a profit. It offers suggestions for creative special events, stories to illustrate how these work, and tips on how computers can simplify all that work.

A successful special event requires organization, adequate staff and volunteers, a realistic budget, lots of patience, and hard work. By reading this book and using the tools it provides, you should be able to figure out if your group can handle a special event right now, and what you can spend on it. If you decide to produce one, this book will be your constant companion as you tackle the business of special events.

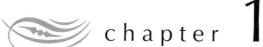 chapter 1

FINDING AN EVENT THAT FITS

Creating a special event is like baking a cake. First, you decide what to bake, then you check the list of ingredients and gather them. When you've got everything you need, you start baking. Special events work much the same way. First decide why you want to stage one. The main reasons are usually to raise money, raise the organization's profile, gain members—or all three.

Next, decide whom you want to attract. Who shows up depends on what type of program you plan. If your goal is to attract a variety of ages, pick an event with broad appeal. You will want a mix, since older people are often able to make larger contributions, while younger ones keep the organization growing. If you cannot design one event for everyone, hold separate events aimed at different age groups—perhaps a dinner dance with a big band for older people, a walk- or bike-a-thon for the 25- to 45-year-olds, and a club opening with live music for younger people.

Take time to figure out an event that is going to be fun and interesting to the people you want to attract. You may want to develop a new idea that exactly fits your particular audience.

One sure-fire special event with broad appeal is a chocolate festival. You can raise money through the admission fee, raffling chocolate goodies, and a celebrity dunk tank. Events such as this can raise upwards of $25,000.

Dinners and dances are by far the most common fundraisers, but such conventional events are losing their appeal and are expensive to put on. In the late '90s, people have developed a taste for parties with unusual themes or promotions, rather than the traditional sit-down dinners with a lot of speeches. Auctions featuring celebrities and their belongings were hot in 1996, with guests bidding big bucks for star memorabilia or a chance to make a TV or movie appearance. These events are lucrative because those who attend have fun—and people who are having fun tend to spend freely.

For example, a November 1995 *People* magazine reported that Erlene Lewis, a sixty-year-old grandmother, thought eighteen-year-old actor Ryan Francis (of the now-defunct TV show *Sisters*) was so cute that she paid $450 for a date with him at a Big Brothers of Greater Los Angeles bachelor auction. He was one of thirty-seven men who offered themselves for dates to support the charity.

While some long-running events might have lost their charm, don't immediately dismiss them. With some imagination and hard work, events such as a-thons can reap serious money for your group. Two impressive examples include:

The Penn State Dance Marathon, among the largest student-run philanthropic events in the nation, has raised more than $11 million since it began in 1972. The money goes to the Four Diamonds Fund for families of children with cancer who undergo treatment at the Hersey Medical Center of Pennsylvania.

In 1997, THON, as it is called, raised $1.5 million through the participation of 540 students who danced (or at least remained on their feet) for 48 hours, 200 student organizations, 2,500 committee members, six major sponsors and thousands of contributors, reports Alyssa Cherkin, the 1997 chair of THON.

The entry fee is $520 per couple. Participants spent three and a half months going door to door and standing on street corners signing up donors. The two pairs of top money raisers brought in more than $100,000 each. The major sponsors — including AT&T, MasterCard International, and the Penn State Alumni Association — contributed $96,000.

In the spring of 1997, Brandon Cauff, a 17-year-old student at Gulliver Preparatory School in Miami, helped raise more than $40,000 for Project: New Born, which funds the University of Miami/Jackson Memorial Hospital's Neonatal Intensive Care Unit.

When Cauff learned of the charity's need for funds, he researched the work done by Project: New Born, met with the executive director and visited the hospital unit. Then he organized a virtually no-cost fundraiser that tapped into interests of his peer group as well as those of the broader community.

His event: a skate-a-thon, with some 300 skaters supported by companies and individuals. The skating rink donated its facilities and hundreds of students sought pledges. The event earned enough to pay for one freestanding neonatal support unit.

Remember, to pull off even a moderate-scale event requires a good idea and the people and money to execute it. Even the simplest events require invitations, a location, and all sorts of incidentals that add up quickly.

Marketing

The key to success is to know what the public wants and what you can do to give it to them. That is where market research comes in. Market research is every bit as important to charities as it is to for-profit businesses. You have to make a profit, just like any other business, or you will be forced to close down.

Apply the same rules of operation to your charity that you would to any other financial undertaking. Long before you decide to stage an event, assess your community, its tastes and spending habits. Knowing your market will make all of your events more successful.

Look closely at your organization.

- How big a volunteer base do you have?
- How much experience does the group have at fundraising?
- What events have you run successfully before? Who attended?
- What other charity events have been highly successful in your area?
- How much access do you have to corporate sponsors?
- Do you need to raise money, or is exposure more important for your cause right now?
- Have you successfully conveyed to the public why your cause is worthwhile and deserves support?

Besides fundraising events, implement a regular program of news releases and radio and television public service announcements. You can tie in to local cable shows and even use the Internet and e-mail to get the word out about your group's cause, goals, and accomplishments.

Member-building activities also require marketing. Your approach could include holding periodic seminars for the public, sponsoring a support group, or hosting small gatherings at members' homes to introduce ever more people to your cause.

And don't forget the World Wide Web. Developing your own Web page can help many people, especially younger ones, find out about you.

Do these things regularly to keep your organization visible. That way, when you hold fundraisers, you can concentrate on raising money without having to spend a lot of time educating people about your charity.

When you set out to raise money, you are selling more than your group's image. You are selling a product—usually tickets. For a first-time event, choose one that area residents would attend even if it weren't for charity. That makes promotion easier. It also helps if you have something unusual planned, such as a high-profile guest speaker or entertainer, or an unusual setting or theme dinner.

If you were going to launch a new product, you would try it out on a few people to see if they liked it enough to buy it. Do the same thing with an event. Take a fact sheet—one that lists the who, what, where, and why of the event you are considering—and circulate it to people you know. Ask their opinions. Would they attend? If not, what would you need to change in order for them to attend? How much would they be willing to pay?

One way to ensure attendance is to take advantage of something that you know is in demand. That is what the Central Park Conservancy did by combining a spectacular location, big-name celebrities who were helping to raise money for the charity, and coverage by a national magazine, then limiting the number of tickets. It brought together *60 Minutes'* Morley Safer, Steve Kroft, Ed Bradley, and Andy Rooney, added Peter Jennings and Charlie Rose, and gave a "Blue Moon Gala" at New York's renowned Tavern on the Green. The event, which attracted 750 socialites, featured the Tavern dressed with 600,000 sapphire lights, and entertainment such as fire-breathers, magicians, an all-blue fashion show, fireworks, and the Mambo Kings in concert. The event raised $2.7 million.

Another example of innovation was the "Women Who Lead" luncheon held at The Breakers Hotel, an opulent Palm Beach resort. Rather than sit home and watch Sally Jessy Raphael on television, participants could see her in person and have lunch, too. Also featured were other outstanding women such as Phyllis Diller, Dolores Hope, and Celia Lipton Farris. The opportunity to hear these women discuss personal thoughts on how women succeed was quite a draw. The luncheon netted $200,000 because virtually everything was underwritten. For a lunch event, that is an impressive amount of money.

Check the society pages of newspapers, magazines like *People, Us, Entertainment Weekly, Town & Country,* and *In Style,* and TV shows such as *Entertainment Tonight* and E's *Gossip* for event ideas and creative fundraising approaches. They also provide information on which celebrities and corporations actively support such efforts.

Sample Events

Following are some fundraising ideas (listed alphabetically). Each idea includes some of the pros and cons involved, an estimate of the staff and planning time needed, costs considerations particular to the event, and the possible earnings.

For an estimate of costs you'll need to complete a preliminary budget. Use the worksheet on pages 24–26. Make sure you include the special cost considerations for the event you are assessing listed in this chapter. Completing the budget is essential for determining whether the event is within your means. There are many variables: cost of location, potential attendance, the strength and organization of your group, whether it's a first-time event, how much underwriting you get, etc. Don't forget to include costs for all the types of insurance you might need: liability, fire, inclement weather, or others.

Working up a preliminary budget will also help you determine your needs in terms of staff and volunteers. Count the number of committees you have and the tasks each one must complete. Decide how many people should be on each committee to complete the required amount of work. Add ten percent to your total number of required people, so that work loads won't be overwhelming and there will be enough workers even if a few turn out to be unproductive.

The earnings potential for each of the events listed below is an estimate based on the amounts

For a successful arts and crafts show it's important to establish vendor rules early on. This vendor application is a good example of how to do so.

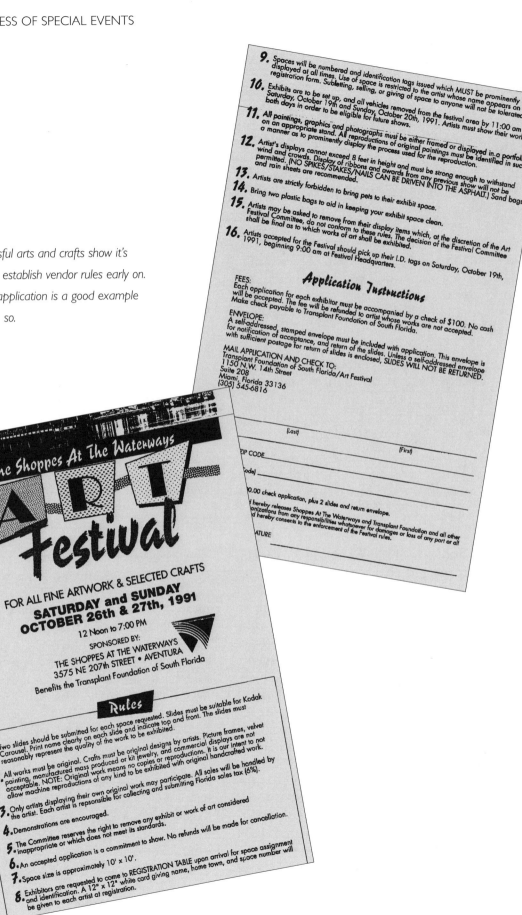

9. Spaces will be numbered and identification tags issued which MUST be prominently displayed at all times. Use of space is restricted to the artist whose name appears on the registration form. Subletting, selling, or giving of space to anyone will not be tolerated.

10. Exhibits are to be set up, and all vehicles removed from the festival area by 11:00 am Saturday, October 19th and Sunday, October 20th, 1991. Artists must show their work both days in order to be eligible for future shows.

11. All paintings, graphics and photographs must be either framed or displayed in a portfolio on an appropriate stand. All reproductions of original paintings must be identified in such a manner as to prominently display the process used for the reproduction.

12. Artist's displays cannot exceed 8 feet in height and must be strong enough to withstand wind and crowds. Display of ribbons and awards from any previous show will not be permitted. (NO SPIKES/STAKES/NAILS CAN BE DRIVEN INTO THE ASPHALT.) Sand bags and rain sheets are recommended.

13. Artists are strictly forbidden to bring pets to their exhibit space.

14. Bring two plastic bags to aid in keeping your exhibit space clean.

15. Artists may be asked to remove from their display items which, at the discretion of the Art Festival Committee, do not conform to these rules. The decision of the Festival Committee shall be final as to which works of art shall be exhibited.

16. Artists accepted for the Festival should pick up their I.D. tags on Saturday, October 19th, 1991, beginning 9:00 am at Festival Headquarters.

Application Instructions

FEES:
Each application for each exhibitor must be accompanied by a check of $100. No cash will be accepted. The fee will be refunded to artist whose works are not accepted. Make check payable to Transplant Foundation of South Florida.

ENVELOPE:
A self-addressed, stamped envelope must be included with application. This envelope is for notification of acceptance, and return of the slides. Unless a self-addressed envelope with sufficient postage for return of slides is enclosed, SLIDES WILL NOT BE RETURNED.

MAIL APPLICATION AND CHECK TO:
Transplant Foundation of South Florida/Art Festival
1150 N.W. 14th Street
Suite 208
Miami, Florida 33136
(305) 545-6816

(Last)   (First)

ZIP CODE

Code)

0.00 check application, plus 2 slides and return envelope.

hereby releases Shoppes At The Waterways and Transplant Foundation and all other nizations from any responsibilities whatsoever for damages or loss of any part or all hereby consents to the enforcement of the Festival rules.

ATURE

The Shoppes At The Waterways ART Festival

FOR ALL FINE ARTWORK & SELECTED CRAFTS

SATURDAY and SUNDAY
OCTOBER 26th & 27th, 1991

12 Noon to 7:00 PM

SPONSORED BY:
THE SHOPPES AT THE WATERWAYS
3575 NE 207th STREET • AVENTURA

Benefits the Transplant Foundation of South Florida

Rules

1. Two slides should be submitted for each space requested. Slides must be suitable for Kodak Carousel. Print name clearly on each slide and indicate top and front. The slides must reasonably represent the quality of the work to be exhibited.

2. All works must be original. Crafts must be original designs by artists. Picture frames, velvet painting, manufactured mass produced or kit jewelry, and commercial displays are not acceptable. NOTE: Original work means no copies or reproductions. It is our intent to not allow machine reproductions of any kind to be exhibited with original handcrafted work.

3. Only artists displaying their own original work may participate. All sales will be handled by the artist. Each artist is responsible for collecting and submitting Florida sales tax (6%).

4. Demonstrations are encouraged.

5. The Committee reserves the right to remove any exhibit or work of art considered inappropriate or which does not meet its standards.

6. An accepted application is a commitment to show. No refunds will be made for cancellation.

7. Space size is approximately 10' x 10'.

8. Exhibitors are requested to come to REGISTRATION TABLE upon arrival for space assignment and identification. A 12" x 12" white card giving name, home town, and space number will be given to each artist at registration.

raised by similar events. How much you raise will depend largely on the size and scale of your event and the dedication and talent of those involved.

> **TIP** As a general rule, plan to have one worker for every one hundred participants for an event listed as "moderate" in people needs. Add more for events listed as "high," less for those listed as "minimal."

Don't immediately dismiss the smaller events as unworthy of the effort. It might be more lucrative and less taxing to you, your staff, and your volunteers to put on a small event once a month, making $500 to $1,000 each time, than it would be to spend six months on one huge event that might only make $3,000. This is especially true in tight economic times, when people are less inclined to attend big-ticket balls and concerts and many major companies, your potential underwriters, are downsizing.

Obviously, all the possible events aren't listed here, but these will give you a start:

ANTIQUE SHOWS

Sign up as many area antique dealers as possible and charge each for a booth. Charge the public a small admission fee. Opening-night previews for those who want the first shot at merchandise generally command higher ticket prices. Sell food and beverages.

People needs: Minimal (one person to round up vendors, another to manage the site and publicity).

Planning time: Two months for a small one, up to a year for a big one.

Cost considerations: Because of the value of the items, add costs for security.

Earning potential: $1,500 to $20,000.

ARTS AND CRAFTS SHOWS

These can be small, simple affairs, featuring home-made crafts, or they can be big and grandiose, such as Miami Beach's Art Deco Weekend, which attracts 200,000 people each January. A small show can be put together in a couple of months, while large events like the Art Deco Weekend are year-round projects. Go to other local crafts fairs to give out registration forms for your show or to collect cards from vendors. Use these to create a mailing list.

People needs: A small show can be handled by two people—one to sign up artists, one to handle staging. A large show might require a fifty-member committee, each of whom chairs a smaller committee.

Planning time: Two to four months.

Cost considerations: Money and good public relations are needed at the outset to solicit vendors long before you publicize the event to the public.

Earning potential: $1,000 to $50,000.

"-A-THONS"

Pick an activity and you can make an "-a-thon" out of it—aerobics, bowling, car racing, bicycling, running, rocking, hair cutting, jumping, dancing, kissing, swimming, skating, skateboarding, walking, wheelchairing, wheelbarrowing. Each participant gets people to pledge money based on how long he or she performs the prescribed activity, or according to score (for example, ten cents per bowling pin or swimming lap, $5 per mile run, etc.). The more participants (divided into groups, each with a captain), the greater the amount collected. Remember, though, if it is an outside activity, weather can wash it out. Also keep in mind that many groups use this type of event and it can be overdone. Check to see if any other, better-established groups are planning them. If so, consider holding a different sort of event. These events work best if tied in with newspaper or radio (or both) promotions and tend to grow the more years they are held.

People needs: Moderate. For these events you'll need people to do phone-call follow-up, serve as team captains, and to monitor the event to make sure things run smoothly.

Planning time: Three months.

Cost considerations: Allow ample money for printing (T-shirts, give-aways, sign-up and pledge sheets) and, if your group has no accountant, allow money for hiring a professional.

Earning potential: $1,000 to $15,000. (Some really big events raise millions, such as the 1996 Gay Men's Health Crisis AIDS Walk, which netted $3.9 million.)

AUCTIONS

These can involve celebrities, sports tickets, cars, single people, travel, food, restaurants, etc. Auctions are among the most labor-intensive fundraisers, especially if there are lots of items and you plan both silent and live auctions.

People needs: High. Many volunteers are needed

to procure items, set up and work the room, and make sure the people with money have a reason to come.

Planning time: Six months or more.

Cost considerations: Because you're collecting items in advance, you'll need up-front money for storage rental, liability insurance, and security.

Earning potential: $1,000 to $1 million or more.

BALLOON RACES

You need a number of elements for this one: a big open field, a number of hot-air balloonists willing to participate, good weather (i.e., no wind), a good crowd. A prime spot for this event is a shopping mall site before construction starts. Other possible sites include large parks, farm fields, and backyards of large estates. Sell sponsorships on balloons and charge admission to watch. Sell food and hold a raffle. This could be a risky first-time event, especially if bad weather wipes it out.

People needs: Minimal (two people) if you hire a professional group or balloon club to handle things; high if you do it yourself.

Planning time: Three months.

Cost considerations: To make this event a success, a major corporate sponsor is essential. Sometimes a new hotel or store, or a radio or television station, is willing to pay for the event, with proceeds going to the charity.

Earning potential: $500 to $10,000 or more.

BEACH PARTY

Hold a giant party on the beach with live music. This is an ideal activity for building a young leadership group within your organization. (If you don't live near an ocean, bring in a load of sand and make your own beach.) The hardest part of this event is getting the permits, since most beaches are controlled by local government. Line up some big-name bands and vendors to sell refreshments. The big moneymaker is often the beer concession, so a beer sponsor can make a big difference, especially if the distributor will donate all or part of the beer proceeds to your group in exchange for being named as a sponsor in advertisements. Get a radio or television station to broadcast live to encourage greater turnout. Charge admission.

People needs: High. You need people on the day of the event who can handle security, man booths, sell food and T-shirts, monitor crowd control, collect tickets, etc.

Planning time: Four months.

Cost considerations: The biggest risk is the weather, so include bad-weather insurance in your budget.

Earning potential: $500 to $20,000.

BINGO

In areas where bingo is legal, there are often bingo halls, places that do nothing but run bingo games. In most states, a portion of every session must benefit a charity. Perhaps one near you has an evening's or day's games open for your group to sponsor.

People needs: Minimal if you're using an established bingo hall, though usually a volunteer from the charity must be in attendance; higher if there are no bingo halls and you have to produce a game on your own.

Planning time: Four months.

Cost considerations: Bingo does best with lots of advance advertisement. Allow an ample publicity fund.

Earning potential: $500 to $5,000.

BOOK OR CD SIGNINGS

Many major book and record stores hold signings by authors and artists. This is not a great moneymaker, but signings can be a good vehicle for promotion. You can tie in a raffle, perhaps a date with the author or recording star.

People needs: Minimal. You'll need people to set the date and location, as well as book the author or musician, to handle publicity, and to help out at the event.

Planning time: One to three months.

Cost considerations: Find out if you'll be obligated to purchase a minimum number of books or CDs. If so, add that cost to your budget.

Earning potential: $500 to $3,500.

BUSINESS OPENING

This can work with any kind of business, such as a store, restaurant, hotel, night club, supermarket, or office building. Sometimes you can arrange for the company's staff and advertising firm to handle the details of the event. All you have to do is provide guests who have lots of disposable income. In return, many businesses will pay for printing, ads, giveaways, sometimes even the food. The more successful you are, the more likely your chances are you'll be asked to participate in future openings. If you can't produce six hundred affluent people for a grand opening, don't try this. Obviously, this is an easy and effective event, so many charities want to use it. You have to have a top-notch proposal and the ability to back it up with people and money (and, even better, a celebrity; see Chapter 9, Power of the Stars) to compete against the other charities that want the same thing. Some stores will donate a percentage of first-day sales to charities. Incredible Universe, a large electronics store, gave 10% of opening night sales to the Boys and Girls Clubs. That 10% amounted to $25,000.

People needs: Minimal for charity if the business's employees help, too.

Planning time: Three months.

Cost considerations: The new business should pick up most of the costs.

Earning potential: $500 to $100,000.

CAR SHOWS

These can include any kind of vehicles—antique, vintage, specific models, RVs, sports cars, or motorcycles. You can tie in with a local club of car enthusiasts or with a promoter who will organize the show. Promoters are usually delighted to have you publicize and sell tickets for the show. Sometimes you can tie in a raffle, too.

People needs: Minimal. Workers will set the location and line up a car club or promoter, then supervise and collect money at the event.

Planning time: Three to six months.

Cost considerations: Add money for bad-weather insurance and coverage for the cars.

Earning potential: $2,500 to $15,000.

CASINO NIGHTS

Casino nights can be quite lucrative, but to be done right, they almost always require a professional company that produces casino events regularly. By the time you rent the equipment and hire the dealers, you could spend more money and time than it would cost to hire a firm that routinely handles these and does them well. It is a fairly pricey, but easy event. Basically, you are buying an event. All your group must do is buy prizes, printing, publicity, and sell tickets. In some areas there are casino boats that you can either charter for an entire day or evening or sell a block of tickets (at a higher cost than they ordinarily sell for so the charity benefits, too) for a particular sailing. Then all your group has to do is sell tickets.

People needs: High for casino nights on land that you produce yourself; moderate if you hire a professional company; minimal for a gambling cruise.

Planning time: Four months for an on-land casino night. Two or three for a gambling cruise.

Cost considerations: Booking a professional company to produce the show will be costly, but can be less than doing it yourself. Don't forget a sufficient security budget.

Earning potential: $1,000 to $10,000.

CELEBRITY APPEARANCE (Actor, Singer, Athlete, etc.)

Caution: This is not a good choice for the inexperienced. Finding a celebrity who is willing to appear at a price you can afford is the key to success. Make sure you have a good legal adviser to review the contract, checking specifically for hidden expenses and clauses allowing the celebrity the right to cancel in advance, and an adequate number of volunteers to sell tickets. Groups new to large-scale fundraising might want to purchase a block of tickets to an appearance someone else is producing, then sell them at a higher price, with the difference going to the charity. Boost fundraising by holding a meet-the-celebrity reception following the talk for an additional fee.

People needs: Moderate. You'll need to book the celebrity and location, handle contracts and care for the celebrity, sell tickets, and advertise heavily.

Planning time: Six months minimum.

Cost considerations: You need plenty of money up front for advertising and deposits.

Earning potential: $1,000 to $1 million.

CHILI COOKOFF

Link up with a regional or national chili competition, line up contestants, each of whom pays to compete, and find a place to hold it. To allow the public to purchase samples, you will have to meet health department guidelines, which are stringent. You can hire the restaurant with the best chili in town to serve portions customers can buy. Charge admission and for parking. Hold a raffle, giving away donated prizes. Getting a radio or television station to help sponsor is helpful, as is a corporate sponsor who might pay for entertainment. Hooking up with a bottled water or beer sponsor with new products can raise more money.

People needs: Moderate to high. This is not a job for a two-person office. There must be a committee to sign up competitors and another (larger) one to handle publicity, site acquisition, entertainment, security, parking, etc.

Planning time: Four to six months.

Cost considerations: Equipment and booth rental will be high. Liability and event insurance are musts.

Earning potential: $1,000 to $50,000.

CONCERT (Local Talent)

Like carnivals, concerts more often boost public awareness of a charity instead of raising large amounts of money. They can be held in a school auditorium or church sanctuary and publicized in a school or church newsletter. To boost fundraising, hold a bake or candy sale or raffle at the same time.

People needs: Minimal. Workers will need to book the talent and location, publicize, and sell tickets. Add workers if you plan to hold a raffle or bake sale.

Planning time: Four to six weeks.

Cost considerations: Addressed in full on budget worksheet on pages 24–26.

Earning potential: $100 to $1,000.

CONCERT (Celebrity)

If your group is just starting out at fundraising, you might want to purchase a block of tickets to a concert that someone else is producing, then sell them at a higher price, with the difference going to the charity.

People needs: Moderate, but there must be people selling those tickets; high if you're planning to host your own concert.

Planning time: Six months at minimum if you produce your own show; three months if you sell tickets to someone else's show.

Cost considerations: A lot of money is needed up front for advertising and deposits.

Earning potential: $1,000 to $500,000.

COOKING DEMONSTRATIONS

Arrange to have chefs make appearances at local department stores (in the housewares department), or at restaurants during hours when the establishment is normally closed. People pay a fee ($25 or so) to see the demonstration. Your charity might also get a percentage based on the amount of merchandise sold during the show. To boost income, have cookbook authors on hand to autograph books. The charity might get a percentage of book sales, too.

People needs: Minimal.

Planning time: About three months.

Cost considerations: Sometimes the department

store or restaurant will cover or contribute to printing costs for invitations and/or posters.

Earning potential: $250 to $1,000.

COSTUME PARTY

These can be based on a theme (end of the decade or millennium, television characters, card decks, colors, and so on) or occasion (Halloween, New Year's Eve, Mardi Gras, Christmas in July, etc.).

People needs: Minimal to moderate. You need people to address invitations, serve refreshments, find a site, organize some publicity.

Planning time: Three to six months.

Cost considerations: Printing invitations and tickets, postage, renting a site, and refreshments should all be budgeted.

Earning potential: $500 to $150,000.

COUNTRY FAIR, CARNIVAL, STREET FAIR

Have an assortment of booths featuring arts and crafts, food, and music (appearances by school choirs, orchestras, and marching bands help get more people involved). Volunteers can put together the booths. Other events that boost attendance include 4-H displays, pig or crab races. This event is more a friend-raiser than a moneymaker, but it is a good way to build visibility. If you can tie in with another organization's festival or "-a-thon" (see above), you may be able to raise more money. Sometimes municipalities help sponsor such events, perhaps supplying a park or recreation center at which to hold it.

People needs: High. Lots of volunteers are needed to pull this off.

Planning time: One or two months.

Cost considerations: Plan for booth rental, site cleanup, and security.

Earning potential: $500 to $10,000.

COW-CHIP BINGO

Arrange for a well-fed cow to be delivered to a football field, and divide the field into one-square-yard plats. Sell each plat for $20, and include a meal in the price. Then let the full bovine out to wander around the field. Sooner or later, the cow will drop its chips. The owner of the plat on which sits the splat is the winner of $10,000 if you sell all the plats. Charge admission for non-plat holders, sell refreshments, and give away prizes. Advance expenses are minimal.

People needs: Moderate. People are needed for site

and cow procurement, publicity, ticket sales, and on-site tasks (cleanup being an important one!).

Planning time: Two months.

Cost considerations: Budget in cow rental, printing tickets and flyers, refreshments and entertainment.

Earning potential: $5,000 to $50,000.

CRUISE

There are several choices in this category.

• **Plan A:** A full cruise. Hook up with a cruise line or travel agent to sell tickets on a particular cruise. A percentage of each cruise sold goes to the charity. Aim for a longer, more exotic cruise for older people with more disposable income. Plan a shorter, less expensive cruise for younger people.

People needs: Minimal. The cruise line takes care of virtually everything

Planning time: Four to six months.

Cost considerations: Private parties and shore excursions will add to costs. Add them also to the ticket price.

Earning potential: $1,500 to $50,000. (See Chapter 6, Locations, Locations, Locations, for more details.)

• **Plan B:** Full cruise with special benefits for charities. Most cruise lines offer charities special packages. Through The Cruise Line, Inc., you can often select a celebrity who will mingle with the charity's passengers during cocktail receptions, dinners, and private question-and-answer sessions. The charitable group gets $100 for each passenger who participates in their group, and also earns free berths based on the number of passengers booked. These, in turn, can also be sold. By booking 75 passengers, for example, the group can earn $12,300, including value of free berths.

People needs: Minimal. A few workers will be needed to sell cruises, for publicity, and to keep in touch with cruise officials.

Planning time: Six to twelve months.

Cost considerations: Addressed in full on budget worksheet on pages 24–26.

Earning potential: $500 to $15,000.

• **Plan C:** Charter a boat for a day. Rent out the whole ship for a day-long cruise to nowhere (cruise lines are very happy to do this when they are launching a new, or relaunching a refurbished, ship). Casino ships are good bets literally and figuratively, as are famous-house cruises, where passengers get a look at celebrities' homes from the water.

People needs: Minimal. Your group will handle publicity and ticket sales.

Planning time: Four to six months.

Cost considerations: Addressed in full on budget worksheet on pages 24–26.

Earning potential: $5,000 to $50,000.

• **Plan D:** A meal on board. Sometimes cruise lines will donate a meal to a charity to get potential customers on board. Your group brings in the people, the cruise line does the rest. Remember that this event is limited to the number of seats in the ship's dining room. Add a raffle or mini-auction.

People needs: Minimal. Your group will handle publicity and ticket sales.

Planning time: Two months.

Cost considerations: Addressed in full on budget worksheet on pages 24–26.

Earning potential: $1,500 to $5,000.

DANCE (1950s–'60s, Big Band, Country & Western, Square, Polka, Rock, Rap)

Since no meal is involved, these are relatively easy to do. You need a place to hold it, music (live or recorded), light refreshments, and some publicity. Sometimes a local radio station will serve as sponsor. This is not usually a big moneymaker, but you can increase profits with a raffle (where legal).

People needs: Minimal to moderate. Workers will need to secure a site and equipment, develop and install decorations, get a DJ or band, publicize the event, and sell tickets.

Planning time: One or two months.

Cost considerations: Everything should be donated or don't do it.

Earning potential: $200 to $1,000.

DESIGNER HOMES

These tours can be complicated. They usually require an empty house (generally one being offered for sale) and a number of interior designers, each of whom decorates one room. Ticket prices are higher than for home tours (see below). Designer home tours take a lot of planning and coordination, and they can easily lose money. Boost revenue with fashion shows, luncheons at the home, auctions, raffles, and VIP preview events.

People needs: High. Many people are needed to work with designers, sell tickets, and staff every room while the home is open to the public.

Planning time: Six months to one year.

Cost considerations: Designers pay for room decoration and do the work. Sponsors should underwrite ads, printing, food, and other expenses.
Earning potential: $5,000 to $250,000.

DINE-AROUNDS

Arrange to have three to six local restaurants prepare one course as part of a progressive meal. Diners pay a fee and travel from place to place for each course. A variation is to have several restaurants each offer a meal and cooking demonstration on a different night. Diners buy seats at one or more restaurants. Sometimes restaurants donate a course or portion of a meal, allowing the charity to keep more of the money raised. Add to the funds raised by holding a raffle or auction at the same time.
People needs: Minimal.
Planning time: Two to four months.
Cost considerations: Liability insurance is a must.
Earning potential: $500 to $2,500.

FOOD FESTIVALS (Chocolate, Strawberries, Shrimp, Garlic, Restaurants, etc.)

A celebration of any local specialty food can be reason enough for a festival. Ask area service groups or local restaurants to serve a special dish or two. Charge each group for its booth. People purchase tickets, then trade them in for food. The charity gets a percentage of the money raised.
People needs: Moderate. Volunteers are needed to line up vendors, for promotion, and to monitor the site the day of the event.
Planning time: Three to four months.
Cost considerations: Budget in booths and bad-weather insurance.
Earning potential: $2,000 to $40,000.

FUR BALL

A Washington, DC, animal welfare group held a fur ball, wherein those wearing the furs were the dogs who accompanied their well-dressed humans for a gourmet dinner, plus games like bobbing for bones. This is basically like any dinner except for the entertainment. All dogs must be vaccinated and leashed.
People needs: Moderate. Volunteers or staff will need to secure a site, handle decorations, plan for a meal and entertainment, and be present at the event to supervise and register guests.
Planning time: Three months.
Cost considerations: You'll need lots of security. Consider hiring professionals to supplement

volunteers.
Earning potential: $1,000 to $7,500.

GAY BINGO

This one obviously won't work in some locales, but in Seattle, Philadelphia, San Francisco, Dallas, Miami, and New York, gay bingo games are playing to sell-out crowds. Seattle's monthly games have been held since 1992, charging $10 admission and selling out consistently. Guest speakers appear. Bingo winners get $100 for each regular game, which is presided over by a seven-foot-tall transvestite/radio disc jockey. This event raises at least $8,000 a month.
People needs: Minimal to moderate. Workers need to procure site, equipment, and entertainment. Lots of workers are needed on the floor during the event.
Planning time: One month.
Cost considerations: Don't skimp on publicity.
Earning potential: Unlimited, depends on crowd. Often attracts heterosexuals as well.

HOME TOURS

Arrange for a group of homes to be open to the public. These can be historic homes or several homes in one interesting neighborhood. The biggest obstacle to success is convincing people to let crowds course through their homes.
People needs: High. Security needed in each room of each home.
Planning time: Three to five months.
Costs: Minimal. Advertising and promotion.
Earning potential: $1,000 to $200,000.

JAIL

Members of your group arrest local personalities then have them telephone friends to post bail, the proceeds of which go to the charity. Advertise heavily on radio and television so people will call to turn in their friends for arrest.
People needs: Moderate. You need a lot of drivers going out to arrest people and a bank of phones for the bail-out calls.
Planning time: Three months.
Cost considerations: Addressed in full on budget worksheet on pages 24–26.
Earning potential: $500 to $7,500.

MYSTERY NIGHT OR HUNT

Participants solve a mystery, either by watching actors perform or by going on a hunt to gather clues. These can be simple or complex, depending on your initiative. There are professional companies that produce these and, unless you know how to do it yourself, hiring professionals can pay off here. There are many site options: a downtown area of a city, shopping center, amusement park, empty building, estate, or farm all work well. Businesses might sponsor locations of the items on the route, refreshment stands, and T-shirts. This type of event is a good way to get people involved, since a lot of people are needed to work during the event. This is the sort of activity that tends to grow over the years. Most only break even the first year they are held.

People needs: High if you produce it on your own; moderate if you use a professional mystery producer.

Planning time: Three to six months.

Cost considerations: Addressed in full on budget worksheet on pages 24–26.

Earning potential: $250 to $10,000.

NONEVENTS

Send out cards inviting people to donate money without actually attending an event. Contributors save the expenses of gowns, tuxedos, gasoline, and babysitters. This can be a welcome change of pace for a charity that has a well-established group of contributors and has put on big, expensive, annual events for some time. This is not a good first-time event for a fledgling or lesser-known charity, because you aren't going to generate enough attention and name recognition to collect much money.

People needs: Minimal. You only have to send out invitations and collect/track donations.

Planning time: Six to eight weeks.

Costs: Addressed in full on budget worksheet on pages 24–26.

Earning potential: $500 to $10,000 or more.

PANCAKE BREAKFAST

While this is an easy and inexpensive event to produce, it is more of a friend- than fundraiser. To make more profit, try to tie in a raffle, giveaway, or pass-the-basket. Do invitations by phone or flyer, or use a sign in front of a fire station.

People needs: Minimal to moderate, depending on crowd. Worker will cook, conduct games, and handle publicity, tickets sales, and site procurement and cleanup.

Planning time: One to two weeks.

Cost considerations: Addressed in full on budget worksheet on page 24–26.

Earning potential: $100 to $1,500.

PHONE-A-THON

Ask a local firm to lend you a room with several desks and phones. Have volunteers call people and solicit donations. This is a very successful means of making money for schools. It makes it possible to raise a lot of money from people who don't give on a regular basis, or to encourage regular donors to give more. To do this effectively, you need plenty of volunteers—people to make calls during the days and others to make evening phone calls—and plenty of phones from which to make the calls. Awarding prizes to those who solicit the most money helps to build incentives for your volunteers. Not much up-front money is required, unless you have to rent an office and phones.

People needs: High. The more people that staff the phone bank, the more money you raise. Make sure you have a day crew and a night crew.

Planning time: Three to six months.

Cost considerations: Office rental and meals for workers are sometimes additional costs.

Earning potential: $500 to $50,000.

RACES

If it moves, you can race it and raise money at the same time. Boats, planes, cars, dogs, horses, turtles, crabs, skunks (de-scented, please), rubber ducks (in 1996, the Olympic Memorial Hospital Foundation in Port Angeles, WA, raised $75,000 with a 15,000 rubber-duck derby), rafts, beds, and even the lowly cockroach can race to raise money.

People needs: Moderate to high. Workers will be needed to arrange for site and publicity, monitor the races, and sell tickets.

Planning time: Six months or more.

Costs: Addressed in full on budget worksheet on pages 24–26.

Earning potential: $1,000 to $500,000.

RAFFLE

Sell tickets to win something donated to your group. You need to make sure this is legal in your community. Check with city or county information desks or local law enforcement agencies. (Some groups call this a "special prize program" to circumvent legal problems in areas where raffles are not permitted.) The better the prizes and odds of winning, the better tickets will sell. With high-ticket items (such as cars), it is possible to sell a limited number of tickets at a higher price. For example, 500 tickets at $1,000 each to win a Rolls Royce are likely to sell, because the odds of winning are greater than if 2,000 lesser-priced tickets were sold. Caution: Don't conduct the raffle by mail. It is much more effective when your volunteers work face-to-face with potential donors, as close to the actual drawing date as possible.

People needs: Moderate. A few people are needed to round up prizes; a larger number are needed to sell tickets.

Planning time: Two months.

Cost considerations: Don't forget to rent a secure storage space.

Earning potential: $500 to $50,000.

SIDEWALK SALE

Have volunteers sell candy, baked goods, rummage items, plants, or crafts. This is an excellent first-time event, because it gets people involved and builds constituency. Volunteers can produce items at home or collect them from garages and attics. The keys to success are a good location, enough people bringing in items, and good promotion (newspaper, radio tie-in, flyers). While this sort of event is not likely to raise large amounts of money at a single sale, it can be a solid revenue source if done on a regular basis.

People needs: Moderate to high. Lots of people must contribute merchandise, and many are needed to handle sales tables, refreshments, entertainment, and cleanup.

Planning time: One month.

Costs: Budget in money for permits.

Earning potential: $500 to $2,500.

TELETHON

The best-known of these is Jerry Lewis's long-running Muscular Dystrophy Association telethon. These require tremendous resources in terms of volunteers and staff. You need a bank of phones, television time, people to handle the phones, and publicity. If the budget is tight, consider a cable or community access channel, which costs less. Generally, you should have a professional producer handle it. Altogether, you can quickly spend $400,000 before any money comes in.

People needs: High. Volunteers are needed to handle phones, guide speakers and guests to their places, send pledge envelopes, and follow up.

Planning time: Six months to a year.

Cost considerations: Phone bank, TV time, advertising, and transportation should have generous budgets.

Earning potential: $1,000 to $8 million (this is how much the MDA telethon raises).

THEMED MEAL (FASHION SHOW/LUNCHEON, LUAU/DINNER)

Pick a workable, attractive site, stick to your budget, and get as much of your needs donated as you can. Tie in a great door prize that fits the theme, create invitations and posters, and construct mailing lists to sell tickets and invite people.

People needs: Moderate to high. This event takes lots of staff and/or volunteer time.

Planning time: Four to six months.

Costs: Addressed in full on budget worksheet on pages 24–26.

Earning potential: $250 to $5,000.

TOURING SHOWS

Theatrical performances, circuses, and other traveling shows afford great tie-in opportunities for nonprofits. First, you will need to line up the touring company. Or, for a performance of Ice Capades, Ringling Brothers Barnum & Bailey Circus, and such, you might buy a block of tickets for opening night and sell them at a higher price, with the difference going to the charity. The National Adoption Center hosted a pre-circus gala before an opening of the Ringling Brothers circus in New York City that included a cocktail reception with clowns, celebrity honorees, and a first-rate collection of honorary co-chairs. Another option: Host a special party for major donors or sponsors that features stars of the event.

People needs: Low to moderate. Staff or volunteers will line up the show, sell tickets, and arrange for tie-in fundraising activities such as the program book.

Planning time: About six months.

Cost considerations: Addressed in full on budget worksheet on pages 24–26.

Earning potential: $5,000 to $50,000.

TOURNAMENTS

Golf, tennis, and car-racing competitions are just a few of the popular tournaments used for fundraising. A successful tournament requires a lot of workers to line up sponsors, a site, and promotion. The more sponsors, celebrities, and media time you can get, the more you are likely to make. Up-front expenses are likely to be much greater than for other events because of deposits required for the site, printing, and sponsor information packages.

People needs: Moderate to high. There is a lot of advance work in lining up a site, teams, sponsorship, and publicity. Many workers are also needed at the site the day of the event.

Planning time: Four to six months.

Cost considerations: If you plan VIP boxes for major sponsors, liquor, food, gifts, and other benefits must be added to the budget. This can add considerably to your costs.

Earning potential: $3,000 to $70,000.

Thinking It Through

After developing your list of possible events, narrow it down to no more than three, and complete preliminary budgets on each (see Chapter 2, The Matter of Money, for details). This will help you pick the one that fits your budget and goals. Then figure out your needs step by step.

- Determine where the event will be held and reserve the date.
- Set ticket prices.
- Prepare tickets, invitations, and news releases.
- Make a schedule of tasks left to be completed and deadlines.
- Based on that schedule, determine your people needs.
- Decide what committees you'll need, how many people are required to carry out the tasks, and how many you have available. Don't forget to factor in that some of your people work full- or part-time, have children, and may have limited time to help. If your regular volunteers aren't going to be able to handle everything, ask them to help recruit additional people.

It is vital to consider your own time in developing and producing an event. If you are a development officer or professional fundraiser, an event could consume half your time over a six-month period. If you have an active committee and chairperson, your time commitment may be less. It is important to look at the big picture and decide how much of your time will be needed to hold an event. Instead of tying up your time putting on an event, it might be better to pick up the phone and ask several corporations or wealthy patrons for large donations.

If you are thinking about changing the types of events the group has had—perhaps expanding from small events to bigger ones for which people will pay $150 or more per couple—choose something that warrants the price, such as a dinner-dance cruise or concert with a big-name star. The more fun people have, the more apt they are to support your cause over the long term.

Take a look at what types of events have been successful in your community. Even those that haven't been primarily aimed at fundraising can sometimes be tailored to raise money. Remember that raising money is your primary goal. If there isn't an existing event to which you can tie your charitable fundraiser, consider holding an event that has already proven successful in your area.

Figure out all of your expenses, and then add a bit more for unexpected items. Organizations that set standards for charities maintain that a properly handled fundraiser is one in which the charity gets 60% of the proceeds, with 40% or less used for expenses. While there is no law that requires such a standard, public opinion can be just as effective an enforcer.

One of the classic fiascoes was a 1988 joint fundraiser for UNICEF and a charity called the Creo Fund for Children with AIDS. In the hallowed halls of the United Nations Assembly, a cast of 150 performed the '60s musical *Hair* for a society-studded audience, each of whom had paid $250 to $5,000 to attend. Although contributions totaled $1 million, just $72,000 (less than 10%) actually got to the two charities, rather than the $600,000 that had been anticipated. The resulting criticism from disillusioned patrons prompted an investigation by the New York Attorney General and the New York Philanthropic Advisory Service. The charity not only failed to derive the financial benefit it had anticipated, but also the resulting negative publicity probably had a

> **TIP** Contributors should know exactly how much of what they pay is a tax-deductible donation to the charity.

negative impact on other donations for years to come.

One way to ensure that your charity gets the most from your fundraising efforts is to enlist the financial help of area businesses. Keep an eye out for large businesses, such as department

Comparison Between Taking a Celebrities Cruise for Charity and Hosting a Gala Dinner Fundraiser
(Based on 300 participants)

Items	Description	300 Person CRUISE	300 Person Gala Dinner
ESTIMATED NET PROFIT		**$53,505***	**$1,755**
INCOME		**$30,000** ($100/person donation)	**$37,500** ($125/person ticket sales)
EXPENSES		Estimated Costs	Estimated Costs
Invitations	$4/piece x 900 900 invites yield 300 positive responses	No charge Printed Materials Are Provided	3,600
Celebrity Participation	Selected from our extensive list	No charge with minimum berths booked	Variable Cost
Postage	55 cent stamps x 900	495 Charities Do Mailings	495
Flowers	$35 per table/30 tables	INCLUDED	1,050
Decorations	(Table linens, props)	INCLUDED	1,000
Music	Six-piece band	INCLUDED	4,500
Audio/Visual		INCLUDED	2,500
Lighting		INCLUDED	1,000
Photographer	Fee includes Prints	INCLUDED	1,500
Food, Bar & Beverages		INCLUDED (One hour cocktail reception plus dinner and wine)	20,100 (Based on $65/plate/person x 300 plus $2 drink/person x 300 guests)
Gross Profit for Charity		**$30,000**	**$37,500**
Less Total Expenses		495	35,745
Plus Bonuses		24,000**	
Net Profit for Charity		**$53,505**	**$1,755**

*   Does not include additional revenues gained from shore excursions.
** For every 15 people booked, the charity earns the sales equivalent of one free berth. For 300 cabins booked, the charity earns 20 berths x $1,200 = $24,000.

stores and hotels, that are preparing to open. Often, they are willing to host a charitable event as a promotion to help attract big spenders. Besides providing the location, they may pay for invitations and food. The charity brings in the affluent people the business wants to attract.

Time and Date

Timing is one of the trickiest aspects of special events. You might think you have a great event scheduled for an ideal time. You might be wrong. You can plan the best event of the social season, design it exactly right for your target audience, have access to unlimited funds and human resources, and still have a flop if you schedule it wrong. Most communities have some sort of social calendar or events schedule. Check with the chamber of commerce and tourism offices. If a schedule exists,

check it to make sure the date you are considering is not crammed with several other popular events.

If no central calendar exists, check with places that are likely to host major events—convention centers, big hotels, and any other place able to hold a large gathering. Also check with churches and synagogues to see if a religious holiday conflicts with your planned date. In a college town, make sure there isn't a big sports game or homecoming that day. Check with the newspapers to see if their events files list any major happenings for that date.

If you plan an outdoor event, consult weather experts for the likelihood of bad weather. *The Farmer's Almanac* and the weather bureau are good sources, too. Inquire about weather on that date in previous years. Depending on where you live, you might want to consider whether you want to leave your event's fate to the whims of tornadoes, hurricanes, or blizzards. Obviously, even thorough ground work cannot ward off an act of nature, but you can lessen the chance of problems this way.

Think, too, about what seasonal natural phenomena happen in your community. In Florida, for example, an outdoor event in August is likely to fail. Aside from the brutal heat and humidity, most part-time residents and tourists are up north. By holding events in winter, during the traditional social season, Florida charities reap the benefit of a larger population from which to attract attendance. The reverse is true in the north. You certainly wouldn't want to plan a big event in Newport, Rhode Island, in January, because the weather is nasty and most of the wealthy summer residents are elsewhere.

Besides the time of year, there are better and worse days of the week to hold events. Previews and other small events are best held right after work on a Tuesday or Thursday night, before people go home. If you plan a Friday night event, schedule it late enough so people have time to go home, get changed, and get to the event. On a Sunday, events should be scheduled early enough for people to get home and prepare for work on Monday.

Where you have an event is just as important as when. If you expect 50 people to turn up, don't rent a hall that holds 500. Similarly, a room that holds only 50 is going to be unsuitable if an extra 20 people show up. (Read more on this in Chapter 6, Locations, Locations, Locations.)

Before you make a commitment to do a special event, be sure you have the resources in both people and money to make it enjoyable and financially successful. Read on for ways to ensure this.

And last: Sometimes it is better not to have an event if all the elements are not in place. The first thing to do is to line up volunteers and sponsors. The other vital component is to prepare a detailed budget that includes a worst-case scenario—how much money could the organization lose?—and to determine how many volunteers and how much sponsor support you will need.

Chapter 1 Checklist

- ❏ What is the purpose of the event?
- ❏ Who are you trying to reach?
- ❏ How many people do you want to attend?
- ❏ How many people do you need to make the event a success?
- ❏ Where will your audience come from? What are they willing to spend?
- ❏ Is the event something people might attend if it were not for charity?
- ❏ Will it help achieve your group's goals?
- ❏ Will it interest the audience at which you're aiming?
- ❏ Do you have enough time for the careful planning required to produce a successful event?
- ❏ Do you have enough staff/volunteer support?

- ❏ Can you afford to stage it?
- ❏ Is there an appropriate and affordable site available?
- ❏ Has this type of event been successful before?
- ❏ Are there potential corporate sponsors?
- ❏ Have you checked for conflicts with other major events?
- ❏ Have you checked the weather reports for that date for the past few years?
- ❏ Have you set your day and time to fit the audience's work schedule?
- ❏ Have you reserved your hall with enough time to set up?

chapter 2

THE MATTER OF MONEY

A charity event should operate just like any other business, and just as in business, the goal is to make money. If you're going to accomplish your goal, you have to draw up a plan and conduct exacting research before you do anything else.

First, you calculate the up-front costs and the "people needs" to determine if there is sufficient capital and personnel to make your event happen. An event, especially a big one, can cost a lot and need a lot of people power, often more than the fundraising organization has on hand. While your event might raise a lot of money, if costs get out of control or you can't sell enough tickets because you're short-handed, you can suffer a financial disaster. By figuring out costs first, you know whether you can afford to have the event and what the chances are of making money on it. Sometimes it's better to decide *not* to hold an event, rather than risk destroying the organization's image and stability with a financial disaster. It's also worth considering whether options other than the event you have chosen might be less time-consuming, costly, and volunteer-intensive.

Also, remember that a budget helps you achieve the greatest possible profit by helping prevent haphazard spending, which can mount quickly.

How much can you afford to spend on an event? Make as complete a working budget as possible to give yourself an idea of what the event you're considering will cost. Then look at how much money your group has on hand. For example, if your group has $10,000 on hand and it costs $1000 a month to run, you have $6000 left to spend on an event in the coming four months. This means a $50,000 event is out of your price range (unless you line up some major corporate sponsors in advance to cover the other $44,000; see Chapter 4, The Art of Corporate Underwriting and Sponsorship).

If you don't have enough money to launch the event you want to produce, consider linking up with another charity and splitting the costs and profits. If you decide to do this, be specific about who does what and what each group's financial gains and obligations will be. Write up an agreement and sign it. Among the items it should cover are what, where, and when the event will be; how expenses will be paid; and how proceeds will be divided.

Approach your fundraiser the way you would the purchase of a house: If you use up all your money buying the house, you won't have any money left to live on. Just as you don't want to be house-poor, you don't want to be special-event–poor, either. Therefore, once you've determined what you have available to spend, you then must figure out your costs and how much your organization can afford to lay out before any money comes in.

Locations

After you've decided what kind of event to have (see Chapter 1, Finding an Event That Fits), you should determine where you will hold it. Location plays a major role in determining the event's cost. (See Chapter 6, Locations, Locations, Locations, for a full discussion.)

HOTELS

A hotel may seem expensive at first, but remember that many costs are included in the price. Hotels, for the cost of the food and (usually) alcoholic beverages, may also provide a ballroom; rooms for changing, storage, and meetings; cocktail hour space and terrace areas. Not included are such things as staging, lighting, decorations, special effects, marching elephants, or anything else out of the ordinary. Keep in mind that some hotels are not equipped from an electrical and loading standpoint to handle large-scale stage shows.

Organizers of an American Cancer Society event in Miami will best remember it for the difficulty they had in finding a portable stage, adequate lights, and sound systems less than a week before the event. The hotel's owner underwrote the entertainment, which featured Rita Moreno and David Brenner. The lighting and sound requirements for their Las Vegas–style shows were extensive. However, most hotels, including this one, don't have a stage large enough to accommodate such shows, so one had to be borrowed from another hotel. Then there was the lighting. The hotel manager was less than thrilled watching the sound and light people drill holes in his brand-new ceiling to hang the stage lights.

Convention hotels, which have big ballrooms and meeting spaces, are ideal for larger events and can more easily accommodate big stage shows. Of course, expect costs to be higher.

Hotels often provide a list detailing the cost of additional services, personnel, and equipment. Many have audiovisual consultants either in-house or under contract. Shop around and compare prices. Hotels across the street from one another may have vastly different costs and, as a result, widely ranging charges. When inquiring about prices, make sure you indicate how many rooms you will need for volunteers, celebrities, and setup crews.

In most towns, hotels are highly competitive. If you're bringing in one of the season's bigger events, the hotels will want your business. If you have a celebrity in tow, your bargaining position is even stronger. Push for everything you can get.

Hotels require that you guarantee that a certain number of people will attend. Be careful not to overestimate—it may come back to haunt you. The number you provide is how they determine which ballroom to use, how much food to buy, and how much staff will be needed.

> **TIP** Sometimes you can get free rooms added in if the catering department won't give you a break on the price of food. Also, many hotels provide free rooms for celebrities in exchange for photos of the stars at the hotel.

PUBLIC BUILDINGS

Don't limit your choices to conventional locales. There are unusual locations that can make interesting sites for special events. Museums, airplane hangars, warehouses, and buildings under construction are all possibilities.

First, find out what it costs to use the building and if there are any restrictions. Some public buildings can be reserved without charge. Some conditions can add greatly to expenses. Many unique buildings have no kitchens, dishes, glasses, tablecloths, or adequate supplies of chairs. There are even places that require you to bring in your own garbage bags to haul off debris. And you may even need to hire security guards and a cleanup crew.

Consider this cautionary tale: In Philadelphia, a day-care facility accepted the offer of the top floor of a spectacular office building, the Penn Mutual Towers, for a fundraising fashion show and buffet dinner. The huge open space seemed like the perfect setting. But a month before the event, the caterer called to say the building's kitchen was inadequate for feeding 400 people. He would need to bring in ovens and an array of kitchen equipment, and also supply tables, tablecloths, dishes, silverware, pots and pans, napkins, chairs, fans, and waiters. The charity itself had to find and install a runway for the fashion show. Because the penthouse had a glass dome, there were strict regulations about the installation of decorations, lighting, and sound equipment.

Many of these items had not been budgeted, but the ticket prices had long since been set. The choice was either to have a cold meal or to bring in all the equipment to do it right. The charity opted for the latter, which cut deeply into the money it raised. The site was truly spectacular, but the same effect could have been created in a hotel ballroom and the charity would have netted another $20,000.

CELEBRITY HOMES
Celebrity residences can be good places to hold events because there's always great public interest in seeing the stars behind the scenes.

For example, one of the hottest tickets of Miami's 1995 social season was a gala evening at the home of Sylvester Stallone to benefit the United Way of Dade County. Only 350 tickets were to be sold—at $1,000 apiece. But interest was so high that the tickets were immediately snapped up and, after much outcry, another 50 were sold.

Stallone had been in town for a year and had just finished remodeling a magnificent waterfront estate, so there was a lot of interest in seeing his mansion. Stallone, along with co-chairs Emilio and Gloria Estefan, *Miami Herald* publisher David Lawrence, and supermodel Cindy Crawford welcomed new arrivals in the courtyard. Guests were directed into the house and then out to the terrace overlooking the bay for a lavish buffet. This event raised close to $500,000 for the charity and people are still talking about the night they spent at home with Sylvester Stallone.

In 1996, the United Way celebrity-home tour moved on to the Spanish villa of singer Julio Iglesias, and, in 1997, supporters got to see Madonna's bayside mansion.

CHURCHES, SYNAGOGUES, MOSQUES, ASHRAMS
Houses of worship can be alternative sites for concerts or themed events. An advantage to churches is that many large sanctuaries already are equipped with seating, and light and sound systems, which may not be available in auditoriums or hotel ballrooms. Houses of worship may have some restrictions as to what days and times they can be rented and what types of events can be held there.

Many such locations have an area that can accommodate a simple reception, and this can help you save on expenses and maximize profits. However, if you plan to serve food, check whether there are restrictions as to what food or beverages can be served there.

Composer/pianist Marvin Hamlisch has performed in synagogues, setting his piano up on the pulpit. The Vienna Boys Choir often performs in churches with the house organ as accompaniment.

OTHER INDOOR POSSIBILITIES
There are many other options for event sites. In most communities there are service and fraternal organizations with their own buildings. With some creative decorating and good food, it is possible to stage a fine event while keeping costs low.

OUTDOOR LOCATIONS
Parks and beaches make attractive spots for special events, because in addition to their natural beauty, they often have plenty of space, allowing for several activities at once.

Municipal parks, zoos, botanical gardens, beaches, water parks, and the upper levels of parking garages are all good sites.

But before you commit to an outdoor site, check the costs for licensing, insurance, and cleanup. If you expect to serve alcohol, make sure it is legal. Also determine whether you can require everyone to pay admission, and if you can exclude walk-ins off the street. Sometimes you can close a public facility, but it takes a lot of paperwork, time, and often, political pull.

When the University of Miami Burn Center used a public beach for a fundraising party, it was not permitted to charge admission. Instead, the hospital held a raffle. At each of its street entrances, volunteers asked for $3. This donation qualified beachgoers to win American Airline tickets to anywhere in the United States. Consider raffling a car or cruise, but remember that not everyone may want to buy tickets, and you cannot require them to do so.

Some other expenses you might incur at outdoor spots can include security and emergency medical personnel.

Audiovisual and Lighting Equipment

Lighting and sound can be very simple—a single microphone with portable public address system and a spotlight. But if the lighting and sound don't suit the event, the event can flop. There is nothing worse than having a speaker you can't hear, a singer whose voice is drowned out by the screech of a malfunctioning microphone, or a play in which the actors look like shadows among the props.

There's one sure way to guard against this type of disaster: Budget enough money to hire professionals. This is one of those areas in which you truly get what you pay for. No matter how good Cousin Eddie was at wiring Uncle John's stereo, don't let him set up the sound for your event. Shop around for a pro, taking with you a list of what the performers require (see Chapter 9, Power of the Stars). Prices vary wildly for this.

 TIP There are frequently different rates for commercial and charity jobs. Ask.

If your event involves celebrities or a big stage show with many performers who generally perform in large venues, take a good look at the audiovisual requirements listed in the contract. Be aware that this equipment is often geared to performances in convention halls or stadiums and might well overload your location. Contact the tour manager as quickly as possible and find out the specific requirements for a ballroom, or whatever size room you are using.

Food and Catering

How glamorous does it have to be? Not very. Food should be edible, presented in an attractive manner, and not so expensive that the charity ends up only breaking even, or worse, losing money.

Usually, food is among the biggest expenses. If money is tight, opt for an unusual light menu rather than having an expensive meal. Consider serving a smaller meal, then finishing with a sumptuous dessert buffet. (See Chapter 8, Food for a Crowd.)

Another large expense is liquor, if you choose to serve it. Many hotels require that you use their liquor service. Many charge on a per-drink or per-bottle basis. There can also be a corkage charge—even if the wine and champagne are donated. This can run as much as $10 a bottle. Ask ahead. It is very easy to have your per-person liquor costs equal the rest of the meal.

The best way to save on food and beverages is to get them underwritten. (See Chapter 4, The Art of Corporate Underwriting and Sponsorship.)

A prime example of how underwriting can be handled successfully was the Grand Prix Gala in Miami, which benefited the Miami Burn Center and Mailman Child Development Center. Rather than having the usual sit-down dinner, the charity opted for buffet-style international dining galleries. There were three areas from which the six hundred guests could choose food: Oriental, underwritten by Nissan; European (mainly French and Italian), underwritten by Martini and Rossi; and Miami cuisine, a mix of hamburgers, pizza, hot dogs, Cuban, Jewish, Haitian, and Bahamian food, underwritten by the Cellular One phone company.

In return for underwriting one dining gallery, each company got two tables at the event for its executives, banners with its name in each gallery, and recognition in the program book. Martini and Rossi supplied wines and champagne, the only alcohol served that night. The only food for which the charity paid was the dessert buffet provided by the hotel, which cost $12 per person. Because costs were kept so low, the charity could afford to bring in singer Roberta Flack for a concert following the dinner.

Even when you can't get the whole menu underwritten, local businesses might agree to underwrite portions, such as the cocktail hour. If you have ample hors d'oeuvres and drinks, the meal need not be large or lavish.

Food costs at hotels are completely negotiable, so be sure to send in a strong negotiator to handle this job. Just because you are quoted $18.50 per person for Chicken à la Hotel, it doesn't mean you can't get the price reduced by 20% to 30%. You can suggest that the dish be modified to make it less expensive.

> **TIP** When you talk to the hotel about how many people they can expect to feed, be careful of the guarantee. A week before the event, guarantee 20% fewer people than you have collected money from. When you give the final guarantee—48 hours before the event—make sure you know how many will attend, because this time it is in writing. If you guarantee 300 and only 200 show up, you pay for food for the full 300. Don't worry about having enough food if you guarantee fewer than actually show up—hotels and caterers usually prepare 15% more than the guarantee.

If you are holding the event somewhere other than a hotel, your organization or the caterer must secure the equipment needed. Caterers generally will do this, adding 15% to 20% to the price of rentals of things such as chairs, tables, etc., for providing the service. If your group has a capable person who can handle this job, you can save quite a bit of money. Most communities have rental companies that can supply the items you need. But make sure the person handling the job understands the intricacies of what is needed to prepare and serve a meal. He or she should consult with the caterer before renting equipment.

Feeding Staff and Help

When volunteers work all day setting up the site and you have paid individuals, such as sound and light crew, musicians, etc., you may have to feed them a meal before the event. Be sure you know in advance what's required for paid workers—sandwiches or pizza, and drinks, for instance. See if a fast-food company will provide this in return for advertising or publicity. Make sure the hotel you choose will allow you to bring in food from outside.

> **TIP** Don't forget to budget for gratuities—the customary rate is between 18% and 22%.

Some hotels try to prevent this. Insist upon it, especially if you are staging a big, costly event.

> **TIP** You are almost always obligated to buy the hotel's coffee service. Concede graciously.

Entertainment

Just as important as serving palatable food is making sure people have fun. That's entertainment. If your budget is tight, the best entertainment is the donated kind. If you can't get it donated, you have to buy it. The more complicated the entertainment, the more expensive it becomes—sound, light, production costs, staging, and technical staff are among the things that will cost money. When you hire big-time celebrities, the costs are guaranteed to escalate on every front. (See Chapter 9, Power of the Stars.)

In return for mention in promotional material, your local piano store may provide the piano—and sometimes a pianist—for an event. Remember to budget for honoraria that may be required for the entertainers, and for any transportation they'll need (airplanes and limousines, for instance), hotel rooms, and meals. Celebrity contracts will list these requirements.

> **TIP** Some entertainers require certain brands of instruments, such as a Steinway piano or Fender bass. Try to have the instruments loaned by the local distributor or a major local musical instrument store in exchange for publicity.

Decorations

Many people go overboard on decorations, so this part of your planning is an excellent place in which to involve businesses or individuals in underwriting and donation. If you can afford to hire a party planner, you might be able to create a more stylish ambiance. (See "Special Events Planners," page 23.) The planner is apt to have on hand a selection of props and supplies that you can rent, choice items that you might otherwise be unable to find or afford. A professional planner can also mean one less aspect you and your staff must handle. Budgetwise, party planners may be no more costly than purchasing a lot of elaborate decorations.

Security

Security is important to control crowds, to protect your guests and facilities, and to keep out gate-crashers. It is much easier for a uniformed security person to deal with people problems than it is for one of your tuxedo-clad committee members. A guest who may have had too much to drink (and who might also be a major contributor) will more readily accept a ride home from a uniformed security guard than from a member of the board.

> **TIP** A party planner will sometimes donate work if the party will be good advertising. You might try to convince the planner to donate the work for all or part of one event in exchange for hiring him or her for a larger, paying event.

As with everything else, get estimates. Hire a private security company or check to see if off-duty police in your community are available for hire. The off-duty police are usually more reliable and less costly.

Insurance

Many facilities require you to purchase liability insurance to protect both them and you against injuries that could happen to guests. Liability insurance also protects you in case someone working on props or sets is injured.

If you plan an outdoor event, consider buying weather insurance in case of inclement weather.

Promotional Graphics

The first notice most people receive about your event is either your hold-the-date postcard, which alerts them early in the social season to mark your event in their calendars, or they receive the invitation itself. These printed pieces need to be eye-catching.

> **TIP** Save money by having someone do the layout (typesetting) on their home or office computer. The same can be done with flyers and posters.

Invitations can include corporate logos in return for the company paying all or part of the printing costs. Also keep in mind that many large companies have their own printing facilities or have

An eye-catching save-the-date card is the right first impression.

contracts with printing firms, and they may be willing to have your invitations printed as part of a larger run. (Some companies have their own graphic artists who might also design your invitations.)

When you hire a printer, make sure you check on all costs, including paper, ink, graphic design, folding, and assembly. Make sure the printer can get the job done on time, too. It doesn't help to have beautiful invitations if they arrive too late. Unless you've budgeted for additional postage, make sure the invitation is the proper size and weight for a standard envelope.

Don't under-order. A smaller second run can sometimes cost as much or more than your initial run. In addition to the copies you need to send to invited guests, add extras to send to the news media and to people on the committee members' personal mailing lists. (See Chapter 5, Committees and Commitments.)

And don't forget your other printing costs: media packets, posters, signage, tickets, certificates, plaques, advertising books, and programs.

Again, it is important to shop around. Get at

least three bids on a printing job. Remember that sometimes you can barter with printers. For example, the charity can acknowledge the printers in the programs and other printed materials, and also supply a certain number of tickets to the event, in exchange for producing them.

Publicity

No matter how exciting and beautiful the event you're planning may be, it will mean nothing if you don't get the word out. Next to ticket sales, publicity is the key to hosting a successful event. You can't simply rely on your ticket sellers to do all the work. Dealing well with the news media is absolutely crucial to your cause.

Experienced event organizers can tell you how much impact this exposure brings, especially in printed media that readers can tear out and put in their daytimers or on the refrigerator as a reminder.

Make sure your publicity committee develops a timeline listing when members will need to contact media sources, send news releases, and follow up with phone calls.

The committee should also have posters created well ahead of time and should make the rounds of area businesses requesting to place the posters in their windows.

For good publicity, certain printed materials are vital. Among them: press releases, appropriate photographs, and possibly advertising space. Many newspapers have discount rates for charities; others will list your event in community calendars at no cost. (For more on the news media, see Chapter 7, The Message and the Media.) Other avenues of free publicity include placing posters in store windows, at hotel desks, at the meeting places of social, civic, and religious groups, and on computer bulletin boards and websites.

For larger events, consider hiring a site publicist with specific tasks to perform for an agreed-upon price. This relieves your staff and volunteers, allowing them to attend to many other details. Most smaller groups don't have the resources and/or expertise of a pro.

Also consider hiring a photographer to document the process from the planning stages through the event itself. Pictures document the various phases of your event notebook and are helpful for pre- and post-event publicity.

Entertaining Your Committee Members

In the process of planning meetings, there may be times when you have to take major committee members out for a meal. Occasionally, restaurants will donate a luncheon for a small group of committee members, especially if they are socially prominent and are photographed there. Afterwards, send out press releases to area newspapers, making sure to mention the restaurant or hotel.

Depending on how persuasive you are, you may be able to negotiate with hotels for a certain number of planning meetings that include cake and coffee or lunch. Some hotels will allow you to bring a group of four to six people to taste-test the menu a month or so prior to the event. This is a great way to stimulate key committee people to sell tickets.

Free Tickets

Inevitably, you will need to give away some tickets, but the best policy is to avoid doing so. Often, large companies will purchase blocks of tickets for their executives or favored clients to use. You might request that when they are unable to use them, the businesses notify you so that you may distribute them to the media or VIPs. In this case, make sure that you give credit to the companies that provided them.

Postage

When figuring out how much your postage will cost, make sure you include your publicity mailings as well as invitations. Add some extra money to cover correspondence with the news media (including press kits), key committee people, solicitation of corporations, and ticket mailing.

If you are mailing enough invitations — two hundred or more — you might save money with bulk mailing, by which the U.S. Postal Service allows nonprofit groups a significant discount on postage. However, remember that this will take extra time because you must sort the mail by ZIP code. Remember also that this type of mail often takes longer to arrive, especially around the holidays.

Bulk mailing probably won't pay for itself unless you do multiple mailings throughout the year. The reason is that the postal service requires an application fee — currently $85 — and an equal amount for each subsequent year you use bulk mail. The actual cost of a bulk mailing will vary, depending on how far each item is going. On local mailings it is possible to cut postage costs by more than two thirds using bulk mail. Contact your local postal service customer service department for further information.

> **TIP** Consider hiring a mailing service to prepare your mailing. They are often faster and more cost-effective than tying up office staff or overworking volunteers.

Specialized Costs

Every event is different. You may need to add some special cost categories for yours. A fashion show, for example, may include expenses such as dressers, racks for clothing, makeup and hair-dressing, extended staging, and runways. (See the list under the section, "Setting Ticket Prices," in the next column) A food festival might require extensive tenting, booths, and electrical generators. For a guest speaker, you may need to pay an honorarium. If you have a big-name star, you will probably need extra security as well as first-class transportation, and you may have to pay the box office that sells the tickets.

Special Events Planners

There are many people who can help you produce special events.

PARTY PLANNERS

Party planners are paid to come up with the theme, decorations, talent, menu, and music. They usually charge a fee plus a 15% to 25% markup on all products and services. Be aware that their job is not to raise money and watch costs, but rather to stage a good-looking event. You need to be vigilant to make sure that they stay within your budget.

SPECIAL EVENTS PRODUCTION FIRMS

Use a production firm for larger-scale events that require outdoor staging, lights, gigantic projection screens, stadium seating, fireworks, or crowd control. Production firms usually come up with a theme; often, they will subcontract to get big-name celebrities. They usually work for a fee plus a percentage (15% to 25%) based on costs.

FUNDRAISING EVENT CONSULTANTS

A fundraising consultant looks at the event from a financial standpoint, making sure the event will raise enough money and keeping the expenses to a minimum. Consultants advise charities on creative ways to obtain underwriting and corporate sponsorships, and on how to increase attendance. If they do the job right, the additional money raised should more than offset the cost of hiring them. Check out various consultants' track records before signing on with one of them.

Fundraising consultants often have lists of affluent people and have developed good relationships with them. Fundraising consultants also maintain lists of companies that may help underwrite large portions of events. Sometimes a consultant will oversee ordering the invitations, devise a theme for the event, and coordinate entertainment. These people normally work for a straight consulting fee.

Setting Ticket Prices

Before planning an event, gather information on the area's demographics—population, average age, income, giving habits. Then, before committing to the event, have a committee question one hundred or more people to see what they'd be willing to pay for the type of event in mind. Also find out what other organizations charge for similar events. Make sure the price you ask isn't beyond the means or spending habits of the people you are trying to attract. Pre-event marketing tests will pay off when it's time to determine ticket prices.

Then, after you have all your bids from vendors and can realistically determine the cost of your proposed event, add 20% for a contingency fund. (No matter how experienced you are at staging events, unexpected expenses always crop up.) Also, you want the charity to get at least 60% of the money you bring in, so to create a comfortable cushion, double the figure you think you'll need to cover expenses.

Next, look at the number of people you think you can attract. This can be the hardest figure to determine. If committees are properly structured and their obligations regarding ticket sales are spelled out, you should be able to come up with a reasonably accurate number. (See Chapter 5, Committees and Commitments.) Take that number and divide it into the total expense. This gives you

BUDGET WORKSHEET

<u>INCOME</u>

<u>SUBTOTALS</u>

<u>Seating and sponsorship</u> of $_____ per seat/ticket _____ seats.

<u>Additional Sponsorship</u>

<u>Levels</u>	<u>Purchaser Receives</u>	<u>Projected Sales</u>	<u>Additional Income</u>
Benefactors	$ _____ seats	_____	$_____
Patrons	$ _____ /tickets	_____	$_____
Sponsors	$ _____ seats	_____	$_____
Contributors	$ _____ seats	_____	$_____
<u>Raffle</u>	$ _____ ticket	_____	$_____
<u>Cash Bar</u>	$ _____ ticket/drink	_____	$_____

<u>AD/Program Book</u>

<u>Levels</u>	<u>Purchaser Receives</u>	<u>Projected Sales</u>	<u>Additional Income</u>
Benefactors	$__ _____page____tickets	_____	$_____
Patrons	$__ _____page____tickets	_____	$_____
Sponsors	$__ _____page____tickets	_____	$_____
Contributors	$__ _____page____tickets	_____	$_____
Listing	$__ _____page____tickets	_____	$_____

Total Projected Income $_____

© Harry A. Freedman, 1982

BUDGET WORKSHEET

<u>EXPENSES</u>   <u>SUBTOTALS</u>

<u>Space Rental(s)</u> $_____

<u>Additional On Site Costs</u> $_____
    Box Office $_____
    Site Coordinator $_____
    Personnel $_____
    Other $_____

<u>Food/Catering</u> $_____
    Staffing costs $_____
    Food   _____ people @ $_____ per person
    Beverages/Liquor $_____ per person

<u>Additional Costs</u> $_____
    Equipment Rental $_____
    Food Preparation $_____
    Tables, chairs, etc. $_____
    Other rentals $_____
                    $_____
                    $_____

<u>Printing</u> (Graphics/Typesetting/Layout & Printing) $_____
    Invitations $_____
    Press Packets $_____
    Tickets $_____
    Program Book $_____
    Posters $_____

<u>Publicity</u> $_____
    Publicist $_____
    Photographer $_____
    Media Advertising $_____
    Reproductions/Mailings $_____
    Entertaining $_____

<u>Postage</u> $_____

<u>Music/Talent</u> $_____

BUDGET WORKSHEET

Decor $_____

Audio Visual $_____
 Lights $_____
 Sound $_____
 Personnel $_____
 Other $_____

Consultants/Supplemental Staff $_____
 (word processing/computer mailing)
 Secretarial $_____
 Security $_____
 Ushers $_____
 Support Personnel $_____
 Other $_____

Miscellaneous $_____
 Hotel $_____
 Limo Services $_____
 Awards $_____
 Licenses $_____
 Insurance $_____
 Special Fees $_____
 Transportation $_____
 Other $_____

         Projected Total Expenses $_____

> **TIP** Sometimes people feel awkward about asking friends or corporations to buy tables or full blocks of seats for an event. This defeats the purpose of holding a fundraiser. The solution is to create a "host" table, whereby each guest invites one other couple.

the amount per person you must raise to cover the costs of the event. This is where you decide if you are having a friend-raising event or a fundraising event.

SIMPLIFIED EXPENSE ESTIMATE FOR FASHION SHOW/LUNCHEON FOR 300

Cost per person (food, printing, postage)	$25
Fashion show—underwritten	0
Site rental—underwritten	0
Total cost $25 x 300 people	$7,500

If ticket price is $50, charity raises	$15,000
If ticket price is $75, charity raises	$22,500
If ticket price is $100, charity raises	$30,000

Again, remember to consider the worst-case scenario. You may expect 300 people to attend, but you end up selling only 200 tickets. You may think the whole event will be underwritten, but find only half the expenses are covered. Before forging ahead, you must decide if the event is worth spending three to six months to produce.

Checking It Twice

To double-check that you have anticipated all your costs, take your now-completed budget sheet and mentally walk through the event.

- Where will it be held?
- Do you need to pay for parking? Valet or security?
- What will the entrance look like?
- Do you need props? Balloons? Mimes? Klieg lights?
- Where will registration be held? How many tables and chairs will you need for registration? How many people do you need to handle it? Are they volunteers or paid staff?
- Where are the staging areas? What equipment will be needed there?

Visualize each area of the event, what will be needed there, and what it will cost.

Ways to Boost Income

Besides the price you charge for the event itself, there are a number of ways to enhance the amount you raise. A sampling:

ADVERTISING

Just as big sports events do, you can sell advertising at your event. Sell space on your walls, doors, and tables. Sponsors might purchase one or all three. At the tables, the company's name can be displayed on a bouquet of balloons or on the table assignment cards people receive at registration. Sponsors can provide handouts with their coupons for placement on tables or in a goody bag guests receive on the way out.

BALLOONS

Balloons can complement many events. Have people walk around offering helium-filled balloons for sale. Each balloon can contain a number that corresponds to a gift (which you have had the foresight to have donated, and which is prominently displayed). Set balloon prices at about a fourth the cost of the prizes contained within (if the prize is a dinner for two worth $40, balloons should sell for about $10). Because the value of what's in the balloons is guaranteed to be more than what they cost, guests have a greater incentive to purchase the balloons. Among the items you might want to seek are facials, manicures, rounds of golf, ski tickets, and dinners for two.

DUCK POND/GRAB BAG

This game is just what it sounds like. Get a kiddy pool, decorate it attractively, fill it with water, and get a bunch of plastic ducks to bob about. Before putting them in the water, place waterproof numbers on their bellies. People then buy a duck and get a prize corresponding to the number on the duck.

You can vary this game by matching the "pond" to your event. At a Hawaiian luau, pick plastic pineapples out of a volcano. A University of Miami Burn Center event used stuffed dalmatians (the group's symbol) with numbers on dog tags attached to the dalmatians' collars. Besides the prize, buyers got to take home their stuffed dogs.

In this game, everyone wins something.

GUESS HOW MANY

Get a big container and fill it with jellybeans, marbles, coins, etc. Or fill a treasure chest with money and charge people to guess how much is in there. Or get a huge vegetable and have people guess how much it weighs (no, they cannot pick it up). You, of course, need to know the answer. At the end of the event, reveal the answer and pick a winner from all those entries with the correct answer on them. Split the winnings among winners if there are several. This is a good addition to festivals and other out-door events.

KEY CLUB
Sell keys, the corresponding locks to which are on the (donated) prizes. You can sell keys for donated bicycles, cars, boats, personal watercraft, motorcycles, or even items that don't normally have locks. In this game, not everyone will win.

MINI-AUCTION
Hold a brief auction at a ball or dinner. Get five or six big-ticket items (that have, of course, been donated) and also auction the table centerpieces. Keep it short. If this drags on too long, you will ruin the flow of your dinner, dance, etc.

PROGRAM BOOK
These books can be enormously profitable. Tell potential advertisers how many people you plan to give the books to and something about the type of people who will attend. Sell ads of varying sizes—business-card size (ten to a page), eighth-, quarter-, half-, and whole-page ads. For bigger-budget advertisers, sell a whole page in platinum or silver, and use that color paper for those pages.

Set advertising rates according to size and placement. The back page, the premier spot, commands the highest price, say $2,500. Inside covers could sell for $2,000. Then stack the advertising so there will be something in everyone's price range. Also offer listings pages, where $25 buys a spot.

As noted above, if someone on your committee has access to or the ability to produce the program on computer desk-top publishing, you can cut costs considerably. Try to get the printing underwritten to keep costs low, too.

Guests receive the books as they arrive. Inside they find a description of the program, a discussion of the organization and its goals, pictures from past events if they are available and appropriate, a list of the committee members, perhaps a letter of support

from a political bigwig, and as many ads as your committee can sell.

An excellent example of how to use program books is that of the Juvenile Diabetes Foundation at University of Miami, which publishes one for its annual "Love and Hope Ball." The program book resembles a school yearbook—thick, and with a hard cover. The foundation makes about $500,000 per year on the book. Of course, the ball and its accompanying book have been yearly events for a long time and have built a constituency. Also, the program book committee works year-round, starting the next book as soon as the ball is over.

RAFFLE/DOOR PRIZE
More and more charities enclose raffle tickets with invitations. This encourages early purchases. Raffle tickets also provide a way to involve people who cannot attend your event by selling them tickets for prizes to be given away at the event. Maybe these people won't buy a $250 ticket to a ball, but they might be willing to spend $10 or $20 on a chance to win something like a cruise. (Obviously, you must make it clear that the winner need not be present.)

Other raffle ideas include selling additional tickets during your event. Display the prizes (sports equipment, cases of wine or beer, posters of a cruise or airline trip, etc.). You can hold a 50/50 raffle: People win half the money collected, and the charity keeps the other half (these are especially popular at festivals and other large events). At banquets, you can raffle off the centerpieces, or award them to those who buy the most raffle tickets at each table.

Often, local publications will sponsor your event and include a large display ad in their publications that outlines the details of the event. The ad can include a coupon for the special prize program.

A mailing to local businesses is a cost-effective way to secure advertisers for a program book.

February 19, 1996

Dear Advertiser:

Every year tens of thousands of children are born with cranio-facial birth defects — quite literally, they are born without faces. The cost of subsequent years of multiple reconstructive surgeries to correct these defects can be devastating for the affected families of these unfortunate children. The Catherine Connelly Children's Foundation benefits such children and their families throughout the United States in several ways: The Foundation provides financial aid to families burdened with these medical expenses for their children's surgeries, public education, medical resource referrals, and other support services.

An easy way for you to support this important organization in its effort to help these sadly afflicted children is to place an ad in the program booklet for the upcoming "Gala Evening at Mar-a-Lago" — an extraordinary evening which will take place on Sunday, April 14, 1996, at the Mar-a-Lago Club in Palm Beach, Florida. This exclusive event will be limited to 350 guests. The evening will include a gourmet buffet, a silent auction of unique gifts and services, a raffle drawing for a deluxe Seabourn Cruise, a short live auction of selected exotic items, and a special performance by an internationally known entertainer in the Pavilion of the estate.

The Ad Rate Schedule is included in the Program Booklet Contract. Please use this schedule in selecting your ad. Thank you for helping us put a smile back on these children's faces!

Sincerely,

Mary Hill
Founder and President
Catherine Connelly Children's Foundation

Linda Silver
Event Chair
"Gala Evening at Mar-a-Lago"

Send a simple sign-up form with your letter to prospective program book advertisers.

CATHERINE CONNOLLY CHILDREN'S FOUNDATION
GALA EVENING AT MAR-A-LAGO
PALM BEACH, FLORIDA
APRIL 14, 1996

Date _____

I hereby authorize the Catherine Connolly Children's Foundation to insert the following ad in the 1996 Program Book for the size indicated below:

PAGE RATES:			
	Back Page	7 x 10	$2,500.00
	Inside Covers	7 x 10	$2,000.00
	Gold Pages	7 x 10	$1,000.00
	Silver Pages	7 x 10	$750.00
	Full Page Black & White	7 x 10	$500.00
	Half Page	3-1/2 x 10 or 5 x 7	$275.00
	Quarter Page	3-1/2 x 5	$175.00
	Business Card		$50.00
	Listings Page		$25.00

PLEASE FURNISH CAMERA READY COPY.
PAYMENT MUST ACCOMPANY SPACE RESERVATION.
SPECIAL POSITION SOLD ON FIRST COME BASIS.

IMPORTANT -   This contract must be returned by March 29, 1996. We would appreciate the earliest possible return of your copy in order to meet the printer's deadline. Thank you.

Name of Firm or Individual_____Phone_____

Address_____

City_____State_____Zip Code_____

Signature_____

The above ad is income tax deductible, as provided by law, either as a business advertising expense or as a charitable contribution.
Your support of the Catherine Connolly Children's Foundation is sincerely appreciated.
Please retain yellow copy of contract for your records.

Sold   by: _____

Chapter 2 Checklist

❑ How much cash does your group have available?

❑ How much can it afford to lay out before money starts coming in?

❑ Is the proposed event within your price range?

❑ Should you consider joining forces with other groups?

❑ Use a worksheet to calculate your budget, pages 24–26.

❑ Look for corporate underwriters.

❑ Set ticket prices.

❑ Look for a suitable location that is within your budget and available when you want it.

❑ Consider additional costs depending on your location selection and the type of event you are planning. Will you need lights, special equipment, etc., to serve food or produce a show? Are these things budgeted?

❑ If you will need a large space, shop the hotels for the best deal on facilities and food. Explore underwriting opportunities.

❑ Decide how elaborate you want the decorations to be. Should you do it yourselves or hire someone to take care of this?

❑ Have you double-checked the budget by mentally walking through each step to make sure you have allowed for all expenses?

❑ Consider what types of income boosters you can add to the event, such as raffles, mini-auctions, etc.

chapter 3

MANAGEMENT: THE VIEW FROM THE TOP

Successful events depend on the deft coordination of hundreds of tasks both large and small, all done correctly and on time. Organizing the organizers can be a complex task.

The Event Coordinator/Manager

To begin, you need to appoint one competent person as event coordinator/manager. This person oversees the event from start to finish.

The event coordinator/manager is the person who marshals the workers required to get the job done. The event coordinator/manager's main tasks are to form committees, assign duties, keep an eye on the calendar, and an even sharper eye on the money. (See the checklist at the end of this chapter.)

The person chosen for this job should have experience at supervising events. It can be the organization's executive director, if he or she has the time to devote to it—they should count on needing 50% or more of their working time for at least the three months prior to the event.

If your organization is big enough to have a fundraising director, he or she would normally serve in this capacity. If you don't have a fundraiser and if you can afford it, consider hiring a well-qualified person from the community on a short-term basis.

Sometimes, an economical alternative turns up in the form of a competent, experienced volunteer. Many volunteers have as much know-how as the pros. Some volunteers produce events on a regular basis and grow quite expert at it. To find someone like this, ask around. Also check the social pages in the newspapers to see who is active in other organizations.

Some locations require that you use their in-house event coordinator or a recommended outside coordinator who is familiar with the facility. This is most often the case at historical sites, country clubs, large-scale luxury resorts, and private or government properties.

During the 1996 social season, Donald Trump opened the most famous high-profile estate in Palm Beach, Mar-a-Lago, for charity and other private events. Any group holding an event there was required to use the in-house event coordinator or an approved outside professional events manager. Someone knowledgeable about the site is better equipped to make the best use of it to suit your needs, helps ensure the protection of such an elaborate facility, and gives you a better chance of having everything go smoothly.

Whether you use the facility's staff member or hire your own coordinator, don't underestimate the value of this key position. Don't limit yourself to those already in your group. Look out in the community and, if necessary, beyond that to other cities, if you can afford it.

PICKING AN EVENT COORDINATOR/ MANAGER

If you plan to select a coordinator/manager from outside your organization (or if you're considering naming a group member who has not served your organization in that capacity before), there are some questions you should ask first. Among them:

- How many events has this person supervised before?
- What were they?
- Were the events for publicity or fundraising?
- If they were for publicity, how many people attended?
- If they were fundraisers, how much money did they raise?
- Did the coordinator/manager stick to a budget?
- How much time does he or she have to devote to an event?
- Would the prospective coordinator/manager work out of his/her home or your office?

- What kinds of people skills does this person have?
- How does he/she function under pressure?

Ask for the candidate's references and news clippings pertaining to previous events. Check the candidate's references thoroughly. Ask lots of questions. If you are considering a volunteer, you should approach this more delicately than if you are planning to hire someone. Nevertheless, it is vital that the potential coordinator/manager's abilities be fully assessed before he or she gets the job.

THE EVENT COORDINATOR/MANAGER'S JOB

The event coordinator/manager's main duties are fundraising, promotion, recruitment of volunteers, and general management.

Consider appointing co-chairs to split the workload. This can be a lifesaver if one chairperson is unable to complete a task, and it ensures that there is always one person in charge who knows what's going on. It is also more practical, because a chairperson may also have a full-time job and thus not much spare time. Whether you choose one or two, consider your candidates carefully, with a very critical eye. The consequences of picking the wrong coordinator/manager can be disastrous.

Consider this example: At a 1996 charity auction at Palm Beach's posh Mar-a-Lago Club, the head of the foundation insisted on managing the event himself. He hired an events firm to produce it, but he wasn't willing to let the agency take charge. Instead, he informally invited many of his friends to the auction to handle the various jobs that are vital to a successful auction. He opted not to conduct a training day, which is a must for an event as complex as an auction. Instead of clearly outlining what each of his friends was to do, he simply asked them to show up. When it came time to work, this group was socializing. Not having been assigned anything else, they obviously assumed that their scintillating presence was all that was needed.

As a result, there weren't enough people to register guests, encourage bids, display items, or serve as cashiers. Many people got in without paying. While the foundation chairman was getting his picture taken with the headliner, the auction was crumbling around him. The thirty friends he'd invited to work ended up having their own party. While the events firm staff desperately tried to salvage what they could, the chairman was out by the pool, pestering the headliner. As a result, the charity lost out on income because some guests never paid and others were unable to place bids.

There may not have been much the group could do, since this man was the head of the foundation and insisted on running things. However, this is too vital a position to let politics determine the choice. Your staff or an events management firm hired to do the job are far more likely to take a businesslike approach and produce a successful event.

 TIP Get everything in writing.

Getting Started

Once you have an event coordinator/manager in place, get your entire group together to break the event into components and determine what tasks need doing. Assign people to various committees.

KEEP A NOTEBOOK
To keep things organized, get a loose-leaf notebook with dividers. Label the dividers as follows: time line and assignments, budget, sponsors, committees, correspondence, entertainment, invitations and printing, publicity, accommodations, travel/transportation, program book (if applicable), photography, registration (including tickets and seating), schedule script (an hour-by-hour rundown of event and script for evening), and welcome kit. Add whatever other tabs are appropriate for your event.

The front page of each section should be a checklist of what needs to be done to complete each task. Behind that checklist go copies of correspondence, bids, contracts, agreement letters, etc. For easy reference, one notebook should be kept in the office and a duplicate at the home of the person in charge.

TIP Have a separate page with all your key people listed, their home and work phones, fax numbers, and home and business addresses. Make up the same sort of list of your major vendors.

When you order something, get a purchase order. If you sign a contract, get a copy. When someone agrees to donate something, send a letter saying you will expect the item or money by a certain date. Put copies of everything in the book.

 TIP Take nothing out of the notebooks. Make copies if you need anything from them.

The advantages to a notebook sytem are that all details pertaining to the event are in one central, easily accessible place, and it is a handy reference for those who take over the following year. Keeping a detailed notebook not only helps the next set of chairpeople, but it can also be used when another group needs help with its event. After a while, you'll have compiled a library of reference materials.

Staying on Track
It is important to create a time line, listing every job that will need to be done, the date by which it is to be completed, and the person responsible for it. Set it up as follows:

DATE	TASK	PERSON

This goes in the front of the appropriate section of the notebook. Assign staff and volunteers to each task, and send each worker written confirmation of his or her specific assignments. If you have an office, put up a big poster board or sheets that list the tasks of each committee, then check the items off as they are done. If there is no central location or office, create multiple loose-leaf sets and update and disseminate the information often.

While you are getting organized, clearly establish who has the final word in each area. This might be the event manager/coordinator, a knowledgeable chairperson, or your group's executive director.

It is especially important to designate a leader in groups composed of many powerful or influential people. In some cases, you may wind up with the honorary chairman, executive director, chief surgeon, and town mayor, all of whom are accustomed to being in charge, and all of whom expect to take command. Just because they are in charge elsewhere does not mean they should be in charge of the event. You need to make this very clear.

Financial Control
Get bids for everything. The costs of sound, lights,

SPECIAL EVENT COUNTDOWN

6 TO 12 MONTHS AHEAD

DATE	TASK	PERSON
_____	Decide event purpose (raise funds, visibility, both)	_____
_____	Choose them	
_____	Visit possible sites	_____
_____	Research/approach chairmen	_____
_____	Research/appoint event manager	_____
_____	Form committees	_____
_____	Get cost estimates (site rental, food drinks, sound/light, etc.)	_____
_____	Get recommendations for music; hold auditions	_____
_____	Get bids for music	_____
_____	Get bids for decorations	_____
_____	Get bids for printing	_____
_____	Get bids for other major items	_____
_____	Draft initial budget	_____
_____	Designate someone to oversee budget	_____
_____	Research/approach honorees	_____
_____	Compile mailing list (individuals/corporations)	_____
_____	Check proposed date for potential conflicts, finalize date in writing	_____
_____	Get written contracts for catering, entertainment, etc.	_____
_____	Develop alternative site (if event is outdoors)	_____
_____	Consider pre-party event for publicity or underwriting	_____
_____	Invite/confirm VIPs	_____
_____	List items to get underwritten and possible sources	_____
_____	Order hold-the-date cards or other event announcements	_____
_____	Set marketing/public relations schedule	_____
_____	Develop press release and calendar listings	_____
_____	Select photographers; arrange for photos of VIP's, chairmen, honorees	_____
_____	Pick graphic artists; begin invitation design	_____
_____	Get geographical information on VIPs, celebrities, honorees, chairmen	_____
_____	Investigate need for special permits, insurance, etc.	_____

3 TO 6 MONTHS

_____	Begin monthly committee meetings
_____	Write/send requests for funding or underwriting to major donors, corporations, sponsors
_____	Review designs with graphic artist for invitations, programs, posters, etc.
_____	Prepare final copy for invitations return card, posters
_____	Prepare final copy for tickets, parking permits, etc.
_____	Order invitations, posters, tickets, etc.
_____	Sign contract with band
_____	Complete mailing lists for invitations and list of locations of posters
_____	Finalize mailing lists; begin soliciting corporations and major donors
_____	Obtain lists from honorees, VIPs
_____	Obtain radio/TV sponsor, arrange public service announcements, promos
_____	Set menu
_____	Get writing confirmation of celebrity participation/special needs
_____	Finalize audio/visual contract
_____	Select/order trophies award

2 MONTHS AHEAD

_____ Hold underwriting or preview party to coincide _____
with mailing of invitations; invite media
_____ Assemble/address invitations (with personal notes) _____
_____ Mail invitations
_____ Distribute posters _____
_____ Finalize transportation and hotel accommodations _____
for VIP's honorees
_____ Obtain contracts for decorations and rental items
_____ Confirm TV/radio participation _____
_____ Release press announcements about celebrities, _____
VIP's, honorees
_____ Follow up to confirm sponsorships and underwriting
_____ Obtain logos from corporate sponsors for printing _____
_____ Secure permits and insurance _____
_____ Review needs for signs at registration, elsewhere
_____ All major chairmen to review plans _____
_____ Hold walk-through of event with committee chairman _____
at event site
_____ Review/revise budget, task sheets _____
_____ Start phone follow-up solicitation for sponsors of _____
tables (corporate, VIP, committee)

1 MONTH AHEAD

_____   Phone follow-up to mailing list (ticket sales)   _____
_____   Place newspaper ads   _____
_____   Follow up with news media for stories on-air announcements   _____
_____   Confirm staff for registration, hosting
_____   Write to VIPs, celebrities, program participants, confirming participation   _____
_____   Complete list of contents for VIP welcome packets   _____
_____   Get enlarged site plan/room diagram   _____
_____   Assign seats/tables   _____
_____   Give estimate of guests expected to caterer/food service   _____
_____   Meet with all outside vendors, consultants to coordinate event   _____
_____   Draft script   _____

2 WEEKS BEFORE

_____ Continue phone follow-ups for ticket/table sales _____
_____ Continue assigning seats; set dais head table, speaker's platform _____
_____ Arrange to meet VIPs at airport train or hotel _____
_____ Confirm transportation schedules, including airlines, trains, buses, cars/limos _____
_____ Confirm hotel accommodations
_____ Prepare transportation and accommodations (include flight number, airline, person assigned to meet flight) _____
_____ Confirm special security needed for VIPs event
_____ Prepare welcome packet for VIPs, chairmen, and key staff _____
_____ Schedule deliveries of special equipment, rentals _____
_____ Confirm set-up time with event site _____
_____ Finalize plans with party decorator _____
_____ Give caterer revised numbers _____
_____ Meet with chairmen, key staff to finalize any of the above _____

1 WEEK BEFORE

_____	Meet with all committees to ensure last-minutes details are covered	_____
_____	Finish phone follow-ups for sales	_____
_____	Confirm number attending	_____
_____	Finish seating/table arrangement	_____
_____	Hold training session with volunteers; finalize assignments	_____
_____	Secure two or three volunteers to assist with emergencies	_____
_____	Finalize registration staff/set-up	_____
_____	Distribute seating chart, table assignments to hosts/hostesses	_____
_____	Schedule pick-up of any rented or loaned equipment	_____
_____	Double-check delivery time with all vendors	_____
_____	Reconfirm event site, hotel rooms, transportation	_____
_____	Deliver final scripts to all committee chairmen, program participants	_____
_____	Finalize catering guarantee	_____
_____	Finalize refreshments/meals for confirmed number of volunteers	_____
_____	Make follow-up calls to news media for advance and event coverage	_____
_____	Distribute additional fliers/posters	_____
_____	Hold final walk-through at site	_____
_____	Schedule rehearsals and volunteer assignments for day of event	_____
_____	Establish amount of petty cash needed for tips and emergencies	_____
_____	Pin cashier's check for celebrity, special permits, on outfit you will wear to event	_____

DAY BEFORE EVENT

_____   Lay out all clothes you will need day of event   _____
_____   Make sure petty cash, checks are ready   _____

EVENT DAY

_____   Arrive early (with all your clothes)   _____
_____   Unpack equipment, supplies and make sure nothing is missing   _____
_____   Be sure all VIPs are in place and have script   _____
_____   Reconfirm refreshment/meal schedule for volunteers   _____
_____   Check with volunteers to make sure all task covered   _____
_____   Set-up registration area   _____
_____   Check sound/light equipment and staging before rehearsal   _____
_____   Hold rehearsal   _____
_____   Go over details with caterer   _____
_____   Make final calls/FAXes to media   _____

MAR-A-LAGO EVENT PLANNING - TIME LINE

Date to be Completed:	Task:	Person(s):
2/26/96	Finish gathering committee names	M. Kaiser
Ongoing	Sponsor request letters and follow-up	Everyone
Ongoing	Continue getting underwriting, in kind, see list	Everyone
3/1/96	Layout invitation copy/including auction insert	Completed
3/29/96	Discuss content of program book	Ex. Com.
Ongoing	Check with committee on major auction items committed	Everyone
3/1/96	Order printing of 500 raffle books upon approval	Completed
3/1/96	Order envelopes	Completed
Ongoing	Organize mailing lists	M. Kaiser
3/3/96	Have committee compile mailing list	M. Kaiser
3/8/96	Set up meeting at Mar-A-Lago for event details/menu/A-V etc./security	H
3/1/96	Discuss party decorations/goody bags	Ex. Com.
3/1/96	Discuss potential honoree	Ex. Com.
3/1/96	Set next committee meeting date and location	H/M
_____	Set pre-party preview date and site (talk to Tim about yacht)	H/Lynne
3/8/96	Finalize local trio on music for event, cocktail hour	Ex. Com.
Ongoing	Finalize major talent with contract	Ex. Com.
2/14/96	Confirm airline sponsorship	Completed
3/8/96	Confirm Mar-A-Lago celebrity space	Debra/Lynne
3/15/96	Layout auction insert	_____
3/28/96	Order name tags	Miriam
3/28/96	Final collection of ads for completion of editorial copy for program book	M. Kaiser/Joan
Ongoing	Set up public relations/advertising. Schedule SD&D and others	H/Laurel/K
2/15/96	Select and order awards/crystal	Completed

4/1/96	Order bases for awards	H/M
4/11/96	Set date for addressing, mailing invitations	Committee
Ongoing	Review budget	Ex. Com.
3/15/96	Review program book proofs/layout	
3/15/96	Organize phone committee	Committee
3/15/96	Organize volunteers, host/hostess, auction table set-up, management/cashiers	Cheryl
4/5/96	Phone committee assignments	Cheryl
4/5/96	Produce final list of auction items & arrange pick-up of item or certificates	H/M
4/8/96	Auction catalog copy	H/M
4/8/96	Pick up program books and goody bags	
4/10/96	Review registration/check-in	
4/10/96	Set up computer for name and seating input	
4/10/96	Confirm registration volunteers	
4/10/96	Set up training meeting	
4/12/96	Final meeting with committee chairs and representatives from Mar-A-Lago	

and food can vary by thousands of dollars. Make sure bids are on comparable products and services. If you are dealing with services such as food or lighting, get recommendations from friends and associates, then obtain at least three bids. Pick the bid you like best, then try to negotiate a lower price.

> **TIP** It may be easier to get a lower price if you are planning more than one event a year. If the provider could get additional business by offering a lower price, he or she will probably do so.

COLLECT ALL THE MONEY DUE
It sounds almost too simple to mention, but make sure you collect all money due. The best way to handle this is to collect it up front, but this isn't always possible. For example, when you are dealing with big corporations, it often takes weeks to get checks cut.

Collect the money before the day of the event. When that's not possible, thoroughly brief your registration committee on who has not paid.

Also, train your committee on how to encourage guests to pay without alienating them. For example, committee members might suggest that the person pay by check or credit card at the door. They might say, "We're trying to keep our costs as low as possible so that the greatest amount of money can go to the charity, so it would be very helpful if we could have your payment tonight." If all else fails, have the guest sign a slip indicating he or she agrees to pay. Bill these people promptly after the event.

Don't lose track of or forget about money owed. Getting the money in advance is the best way to ensure its arrival.

It's customary to require a check when people reserve a block of seats. If they don't send in a check, call and ask when it will be coming, or suggest they use a credit card.

CREDIT CARDS
Accepting credit cards will cost your group 2% to 6%. The percentage charged varies with the card and the sponsoring institution, but because they are easy for people to use, accepting credit cards can boost sales.

At an auction, antique show, or "-a-thon," where spur-of-the-moment purchasing is likely

to occur, credit cards can sometimes double the amount you make. At a ball or dinner, they probably won't make much difference.

> **TIP** You can sometimes negotiate a lower percentage on cards (Visa and MasterCard) offered by local banks. The more money you run through the account, the lower your rate. Also, American Express has a special charity rate.

However, there is a down side to credit cards. They can be time-consuming, because you must check to see if a person's credit is good. You will have to buy the machines with which you process the charge slips, and you'll need access to a direct telephone line to use it. Sometimes you have to buy the credit slips themselves. And it can be embarrassing for donors if you find out they have exceeded their credit line.

MONEY MANAGER
One person should oversee accounting and maintain the budget, and take care of banking, purchasing, ticket sales, legal matters, and collections. It is better if it is someone other than the event manager, who is already taking care of many details. If you have someone available who is capable, designate that person and give him or her the sole responsibility of handling financial matters. If you don't, hire a competent bank executive or accountant, or convince one to become a committee member whose job will be to manage the money.

> **TIP** Several days in advance, pin the check on the tuxedo or dress you plan to wear, or put it in the purse or briefcase you plan to carry to the event.

If you're putting on a major event, one of the most important reasons to have a money manager is that many celebrities require payment by certified check on the night of the performance. Forget to bring that check and they will forget the show they had planned.

BANK ACCOUNTS
If you are having a small-scale event, it is not worth your time (or the bank's) to open an account, but if

you plan to have several events or one large one, it may pay off.

Keep a separate bank account for the event, if possible, so these funds and expenses will not get mixed up with your charity's regular funds and expenses. If you accumulate large amounts of money ahead of time, put them in a money-market account to earn some interest. Make sure you know how many checks you can write without incurring charges for doing so.

Handling Ticket Sales

Tickets are the same as money and should be handled as such. The best way to maintain control over tickets is to number them in two places—one on the stub the group keeps, the other on the part the buyer keeps. Use these numbers for accounting. If your members are selling your tickets, make sure everyone gets clear written instructions on:

- How many tickets they are responsible for selling.
- The date by which they must be sold.
- Remaining responsible for those tickets, even if they distribute them to others to sell.
- Collecting money when they give people their tickets.

All committee members should develop a list of people they will approach. Give each member a support packet that includes handouts explaining the event and the charity. Encourage them to write down a brief pitch that explains what the event is and why someone should buy the ticket. If they have a place to post them, give them posters to put up. This can make a big difference in ticket sales.

The tickets themselves should include the name of the event, time, date, place, and cost per ticket as well as the identifying number you use to account for them.

> **TIP** To help prevent counterfeiting, include a special design, logo, or trademark on the ticket that would be hard to copy, or select an unusual paper for printing the tickets.

Keep track of the tickets by number, matching the person who is handling each block with a specific series of numbers. Write all this down in your notebook.

Boost sales by offering prizes to those who sell the most tickets. Many businesses will donate dinners, haircuts, facials, makeup lessons, or rounds of golf. For bigger events, you might be able to offer a cruise or airline tickets. As another incentive, offer your sales force free tickets if they are able to sell ten tickets to other people. (If you do this, be sure you've accounted for this in your expenses or can find a business willing to sponsor the cost of these tickets.)

Give your sales force a list of contacts (chamber of commerce membership lists, "Yellow Pages" listings, etc.) and let your salespeople take the names of those at which they know someone personally. Divide up the rest of your list among your salespeople so they can make cold calls. Make sure you include all the large companies in town, as well as stock brokerage firms, banks, law offices, and hospitals.

For large ticketed events, consider hiring a ticket service. Usually there's only one in the area, such as Ticketmaster. The "Yellow Pages" of the phone directory usually list whatever ticket services there are. For a percentage of sales (usually 1% to 3%), the company computerizes your tickets, sells them, and handles the bookkeeping and payment processing. Every outlet maintains a list of events for which it sells tickets, so you can get added exposure there. Ticketron produces a monthly events publication that it sends to subscribers, and distributes flyers at each outlet. Many other ticket services will also promote your event in their advertising.

For an event at which you expect to sell 2,000 or more tickets, a ticket service is usually well worth the money. Because the committee people will have the names of people who should be sent invitations, arrange to retain tickets on which you won't pay the ticket service's surcharge so they can be sold to the names your committee people have provided.

Make sure that everyone selling tickets knows when they must return the unsold ones to you. One thing that often happens if you're not careful is that you can get a false impression that your event is sold out when it's not. It is important to determine how many tickets have been paid for.

TICKET ACCOUNTING

Keep a ticket ledger separate from the notebook, with copies in the charity office or your event-planning headquarters. The ledger should list each ticket number and who is responsible for it. On the night of the event, make sure you collect the stubs of all the tickets. Later match them to the numbers recorded in the ledger. By doing so you'll be able to see how many people actually showed up and reconcile the numbers with the amount of money you actually collected. You want to get all the unsold tickets back for the same reason.

 TIP Ticket sellers should get cash first, count it carefully, then deliver the ticket.

"FREE" TICKETS

Inevitably, a bunch of tickets get handed out to people who don't pay for them—local bigwigs, the news media, etc. Try to have these tickets underwritten. Give the businesses or individuals who underwrite or sponsor tickets to be given away credit on signage at tables and in the program book, and create a media table, with the underwriters' names prominently displayed.

"PAPERING THE HOUSE"

If you want your event to look sold out even when it isn't, you can "paper the house"—give out free tickets to civic organizations, police groups, retirement homes, and students and others who might not otherwise be able to attend, thus exposing more people to your cause. You can also do this if you have exhausted all avenues of selling tickets and feel you have made as much money as you are going to. Give away tickets only to theater or show events, never to a sit-down meal. Use give-aways only for events at which it doesn't cost you any more to fill up the seats.

Chapter 3 Checklist

- ❏ Have tentative budget and type of event set.
- ❏ Have a working budget with as much detail as possible, including cost estimates.
- ❏ Have key organization officials examine list of potential event coordinator/managers, check each one's references and experience, then select best one.
- ❏ The event coordinator/manager forms committees, then drafts a list of tasks that need to be done, assigning them to each committee along with a date for completion.
- ❏ Start a loose-leaf notebook in which to document every element of your event.
- ❏ Negotiate contracts with vendors, entertainers, etc.
- ❏ Keep an eye on the budget or appoint a financial manager to handle bookkeeping and collections.
- ❏ Determine if it's appropriate to the size of your event to set up special bank accounts. Do so if warranted.

- ❏ Determine whether it pays to set up to accept credit cards. Shop for the best rate.
- ❏ Determine whether to use a ticket service or to have staff and volunteers sell tickets.
- ❏ Keep careful track of who has which tickets. Make sure everyone is accountable to the financial manager.
- ❏ Set up a ticket ledger to track tickets from distribution through payment. Supply a copy to the accountant or financial manager and one to the main office.
- ❏ Arrange to have the tickets that are to be given away underwritten by area companies and other sponsors.
- ❏ Consider carefully when or whether it is time to paper the house, giving blocks of tickets to people who ordinarily might not be able to attend such a show.

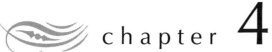

chapter 4

THE ART OF CORPORATE UNDERWRITING AND SPONSORSHIP

For charities looking to maximize profit on large events, corporate sponsors are essential to underwriting the majority of expenses.

Underwriting is any contribution—in money, items, or in-kind services from individuals, businesses, and corporations—that lowers the amount the nonprofit organization must pay for expenses. The company donates items or cash for a specific event, covering costs such as printing, food, entertainment, audiovisual services, and other event-related expenses. The charity reciprocates by including the company's name in print or electronic advertising, on invitations and tickets, on banners at the event, or in other ways.

Take, for example, one group that goes all-out in acknowledging its biggest sponsors. This is the American Ballet Theater in New York City. Its top corporate sponsors not only get publicity in advertisements and in the dance program, but they also get the best seats in the house and a chance to mingle with the dancers at a private reception the night of a performance.

If you were starting a new business venture, you would line up companies willing to help you get things going, to provide start-up inventory, and to support your fledgling venture while it got on its feet. Use that same approach when working on a

Use a letter seeking underwriting to remind established business contacts of your cause and to expose it to new ones.

American Cancer Unit

To Whom It May Concern:

The American Unit of the Woman's Corps is a local volunteer organization that raises funds for the Cancer Research Center at the New York University School of Medicine. The money is used exclusively for cancer research.

We have been in existence since 1932, and today over 4,000 members are working relentlessly to raise funds for important research programs. Every cause is a worthy one, but cancer is everyone's cause. We are all working for the day we can live without fear of cancer.

The challenge is especially critical in New York, which ranks number one in the U.S. in death rates for cancer. As the nationally designated cancer center for the state of New York, the Comprehensive Cancer Center is charged with preventing as many cancers as possible. Work being done at the Center is giving us not only new facts, but new hope as well.

You can help us raise the money so desperately needed for research in one of the following ways:

-Donate a door prize, for a lucky person

-Underwrite some of the expenses of our event

-Make an outright gift to our cause.

On behalf of all who benefit from the research being done at the Cancer Center, thank you for your support.

Sincerely,

Mrs. T. Smith
Chairperson

special event. So, as discussed in Chapter 2, The Matter of Money, once you establish a realistic budget but before you commit to staging an event, evaluate the potential sources of corporate and individual underwriting. The most likely source of underwriting for many events could come directly from members of the event committee, their personal and business contacts, or prominent local business leaders and their companies. But be sure to look at the regional and national possibilities as well as local opportunities.

> **TIP** Check with local chambers of commerce to locate the biggest companies in the region. Then approach the companies for support.

Art Deco Weekend on Miami Beach is an excellent example of achieving maximum fundraising through the informed use of major underwriting. The annual weekend-long event helps the Miami Design Preservation League raise money for numerous historic preservation projects. The committee lines up many sponsors, including at least one airline, a beer company, and a hotel. The airline flies in VIPs and celebrities who will entertain at the show; the hotel sponsor furnishes their rooms. The beer sponsor pays the Design Preservation League about $20,000 for the exclusive right to sell beer at the well-attended event. That money is used to help pay for cleanup, printing posters, and providing sound and lights. The League also sells booths to exhibitors, who sell their wares there. The income from booth sales pays for the tents and booths. The League clears between $50,000 and $75,000 from selling booths. In addition, the Design Preservation League operates its own booth, selling art deco posters, T-shirts, and gifts, which raises still more money.

A $100-per-person ball kicks off the weekend with top-40 music and an antique car parade. Weekend promotion appears in national magazines, television commercials, and in regional mailings by the Miami Beach Visitors and Convention Bureau.

Sponsors wind up getting a return of three to four times their underwriting dollar investment in national exposure.

Media First

A good way to start the search for underwriting is to secure a radio station or newspaper—or both—as a sponsor. Generally, the media will give you a certain amount of advertising time/space to promote your event. With the media on board, it's easier to line up sponsorship from other businesses interested in promoting themselves while supporting a worthwhile cause.

When you're looking for a radio station's support, pick a station whose listeners are the type of people you want to attract to your event. All radio stations can tell you precisely who their listeners are—their ages, median incomes, and listening habits. This is the information they use to sell commercials. Ask to see and examine their demographics. For a chili festival promotion, you might go to a country-and-western station, whose listeners are likely to consist of a wide age group and working-class families—people who are most likely to attend the event.

> **TIP** Radio stations are likely to be more receptive to a charity's request for public service announcements if the charity can offer the station paying commercials from its corporate-sponsor partners.

If anyone in your group knows someone influential at a newspaper, radio, or television station, request that the member contact that person to let him or her know someone from your group will be calling to seek support for a charitable cause. This can help pave the way.

Don't forget that community calendars on radio, television, newspapers, magazines, and the Internet are generally free.

Getting Maximum Support

How many sponsors are there with deep pockets? A report by International Events Group (IEG) shows that the country's 1,800 most active corporate sponsors distribute $5 billion in underwriting annually to get their names out through event sponsorship. So keep in mind that there's a big pool of money out there, and some of it might head your way if you ask for it.

To obtain sponsorship from a national company, an event must draw at least 2,500 people. Corporate sponsors require you to give them the demographics of those attending as well, so make sure that information is available before you make your request.

In seeking major corporate or title sponsorship for an event, enumerate exactly what is expected of the sponsor and what it gets in return – just like you would for any other joint business venture.

actionAIDS

Care in Action

1216 Arch Street
Philadelphia, PA 19107
Telephone: 215 981 0088
Fax: 215 864 6930

Kevin R. Conare
Executive Director

Board of Directors
David S. Blum, Esq.
President
Oliver Jordan
Vice President
Dean Vance, C.P.A.
Treasurer
Chrissa B. Merron
Secretary

Marjorie H. Adler
William Cody Anderson
Andrew A. Barasda, Jr.
David W. Brown
Dawna R. Edwards
Judi Erlichman-Rothaus
Jim Fennell

Sandra Fletcher
George Gates
The Hon. W. Wilson Goode
Dale L. Grundy
Joseph H. Huston, Jr.
Paul N. Kelly, C.P.A.
Karl S. Krumholz, AIA

Alice Marini
Shawn Mott
Linda Newkirk-Davenport
I. Thomas Odrick, Jr.
Pedro J. Rivera, Esq.
Mark B. Woodland, M.D.

Community Offices:
3901 Market Street, Box 1934, Philadelphia, PA 19104
2718 North 5th Street, Philadelphia, PA 19133

http://www.critpath.org/actionaids
TDD: Use PA Relay System

SAMPLE SPONSOR REQUEST COVER LETTER

October 22, 1997

Mr. David Smith
Senior Vice President
Public Affairs & Government Banking
FIRST NATIONAL BANK
Broad Street
Philadelphia, Pennsylvania 19100

Dear Mr. Smith,

Enclosed please find a packet for sponsorship of *Dining Out for Life 1998*. This is an excellent promotional opportunity for your company's public affairs division to support, as a $15,000 Title Sponsor, a fundraising event which uses "solid business practices" to raise money for educational and service programs in the tri-state region. This program is a "win-win" situation for both your company and the non-profit organizations that will receive the funds raised through this event.

In Philadelphia, corporate sponsors can receive (based on level of participation):
 - corporate name inclusion on 90,000 printed materials
 - up to $146,000 in direct advertising and promotional benefits
 - use of event related fundraising mailing lists
 - specifically tailored promotions at participating restaurants
Through your sponsorship of this event, corporate visibility will be greatly increased well beyond usual advertising methods.

The fundraising results from the last three years' *Dining Out* events have been so successful that *Dining Out '98* is being implemented simultaneously in twenty-four additional cities on March 12, 1998. This event will be the first international cooperative effort to raise funds in the massive battle against AIDS and related HIV spectrum diseases.

Page Two

I became involved with *Dining Out '98* to maximize fundraising efforts with the goal of raising $46,450 to underwrite all event related expenses. With these expenses underwritten, 100% of the funds raised will go directly to provide services and educational programs.

I recently returned to my hometown of Philadelphia after over 15 years in Florida. I have earned a national reputation as a builder of partnerships between businesses and charities. I have advised hundreds of charitable organizations on how to raise significant funds while controlling expenses. Large national companies and retail businesses often seek my advice to increase their target markets through involvement with regional and national charitable causes.

During the next several months, I will be personally working with several major charities to help them secure sponsors for various events. I anticipate contacting regional companies for support only when I feel there is a good match. When appropriate, I hope to encourage the organizations, I consult with, to broaden their base of support beyond traditional funding sources.

I would greatly appreciate the opportunity to briefly meet with you so I may become more familiar with your corporate charitable giving policy, philosophy and marketing support through event sponsorships. With this information, I could certainly help to reduce some of inappropriate proposals being submitted to you.

Thank you again for your consideration to join our other corporate sponsors in support of Dining Out for Life 1998.

Sincerely,

Harry A. Freedman
Sponsorship Advisor

DINING OUT FOR LIFE® 1998 SPONSORSHIP OPPORTUNITIES

Dining Out for Life® is a unique fundraiser, created by ActionAIDS, which invites restaurants to contribute a portion of their business to AIDS service organizations on one day each year. In its seven year history, Dining Out for Life® has grown both locally and nationally. In 1998, over 170 local restaurants and 25,000 diners are expected to participate in Philadelphia's Dining Out for Life®. Funds raised through the event will support ActionAIDS, the AIDS Coalition of Southern New Jersey, AIDS Delaware, Planned Parenthood of Chester County, and Project Hope of Montgomery County. In addition to revenue from restaurant contributions, Dining Out for Life® benefits from the donations of individual diners on the day of the event.

In 1998, for the first time, Dining Out for Life® will take place in more than 25 cities throughout North America on the same day. More than one million people are expected to participate throughout the United States and Canada.

> **Summary:**
>
> Philadelphia
> Dining Out for Life®
>
> Thursday, March 12, 1998
> Expected Attendance:
> 25,000
>
> Will take place in restaurants throughout the city and suburbs.
>
> International
> Dining Out for Life®
>
> Expected Attendance:
> 1,000,000
>
> Will take place in more than 25 North American cities.

Dining Out for Life® Philadelphia Revenue

Previous Sponsors of Dining Out for Life®

American Airlines
American Express Financial Advisors
Continental Airlines
Greater Media Cable
Health Partners
Kahlua & Cream
Philadelphia Bar Association,
Young Lawyers Division
Philadelphia City Paper
Travel Now
The Wall Music
Way to Go Costa Rica

Advertising and Promotions

SPONSORS CAN RECEIVE UP TO $146,000 IN ADVERTISING.

Print Advertising

Daily Publications: **$13,000 in paid advertising = 12 insertions**

(Includes the Philadelphia Inquirer, Daily News, Camden Courier Post and Montgomery Newspapers.)

Weekly/Monthly Publications:
$5,000 in paid advertising
$15,000 in-kind advertising

$20,000 advertising = 20 insertions

(Includes a special Dining Out for Life® insert in the Philadelphia City Paper and advertising in the Philadelphia Gay News, the Jewish Exponent and Philadelphia Magazine.)

Television Advertising

PSA placement with a minimum frequency level of three spots per day on the sponsoring station for a one-month period leading up to the event.

$72,999 in-kind advertising = 90 spots/ month

Radio

Celebrity DJ's announce their participation and chat with local restaurateurs.

$40,000 in-kind advertising = 200 spots/month

World Wide Web

Dining Out for Life® home page will be available from mid-December until the event and will list all sponsors and participating restaurants. (Address: http://www.critpath.org/actionaids/dev/dol.htm).

Editorial Support

Dining Out for Life® receives substantial print and media placement each year, courtesy of daily and community publications as well as television and radio stations. Following is a sampling of the organizations that provided advertising and articles for Dining Out for Life® in 1996 and 1997:

Bucks County Courier Times	*Main Line Times*	*Philadelphia Inquirer*
Chestnut Hill Local	*Montgomery Newspapers*	*Au Courant*
Philadelphia Daily News	*Northeast Times*	*Ritz Filmbill*
Daily Pennsylvanian	*Philadelphia City Paper*	*WPVI-TV 6*
Delaware County Daily Times	*Philadelphia Gay News*	

$15,000 TITLE SPONSOR

Receives:
- name recognition at the top of all printed materials and mention in all media promotions as the presenter of Philadelphia's Dining Out for Life®
- corporate logo inclusion as title sponsor on 90,000 printed materials
- corporate name/logo inclusion on all PSA's, radio, television, print and outdoor advertising
- product and/or signage presence at the Dining Out for Life® media kick-off event
- endorsement as title sponsor from ActionAIDS to all participating restaurants
- product material distribution by volunteers to 10,000 diners in at least 100 participating restaurants during Dining Out for Life®

The Title Sponsor enables ActionAIDS to apply 80% of the event's revenue directly to services for people with HIV disease by covering the costs of printing all materials.

$7,500 PRIMARY SPONSOR

Receives:
- corporate name inclusion on 90,000 printed materials
- corporate name inclusion on all PSA's for radio and television and outdoor advertising
- logo inclusion on 10,000 Dining Out for Life® table tents appearing on each table of every local participating restaurant for one month prior to the event

Primary Sponsors enable ActionAIDS to apply event revenue directly to services for people with HIV disease by supporting the costs of advertising.

$4,000 SPONSOR

Receives:
- corporate name inclusion on 45,000 Dining Out for Life® event postcards
- corporate name inclusion on 4,200 Dining Out for Life® posters

Sponsors enable ActionAIDS to apply event revenue directly to services for people with HIV disease by supporting postage costs for Dining Out for Life®, including the mailing of event postcards to over 45,000 potential diners.

MEDIA SPONSOR

Receives:
- corporate name inclusion on 90,000 printed materials
- corporate name inclusion on all PSA's for radio, television and outdoor advertising
- logo inclusion on 10,000 Dining Out for Life® table tents appearing on each table of every local participating restaurant for one month prior to the event

The Media Sponsor enables ActionAIDS to apply event revenue directly to services for people with HIV disease by donating media advertising and promotional space.

ActionAIDS Dining Out for Life® 1998 Budget

Expenses:

Advertising	$18,000
Printing	15,000
Postage	6,000
Insurance	3,200
Suburban Beneficiaries	3,000
Supplies	1,200
Telephone	50
TOTAL EXPENSES:	$46,450
PROJECTED REVENUE:	$158,000
PROJECTED NET:	$111,550

Dining Out for Life® Promotional Materials

The Title and Primary Sponsors' names/logos appear on all promotional materials, including:

Event Postcards	35,000 mailed to ActionAIDS donor list 10,000 distributed elsewhere
Table Tents	10,000 continuously displayed on each table of every local participating restaurant for one month
"All Year Round" Cards	20,000 distributed to participating diners
Event Posters	3,500 distributed throughout Philadelphia, Chester, and Montgomery Counties, and southern New Jersey 200 displayed in participating restaurants and sponsoring organizations
Event Flyers	10,000 distributed to community business and relevant organizations

ActionAIDS
Organizational Information

ActionAIDS is a nonprofit, community-based organization founded in 1986 to meet the physical and emotional needs of men, women and children affected by HIV and AIDS. Last year, ActionAIDS served over a quarter of all people living with AIDS in Philadelphia. The agency annually provides services to approximately 2,500 individuals and 100 families at 13 locations throughout the city, including four prisons, and presently has a waiting list of 108 people who qualify for service but cannot be accommodated due to financial limitations.

Now in its eleventh year of operation, with over 65 staff members, 500 volunteers, and a budget of almost $3.5 million, ActionAIDS is Pennsylvania's largest AIDS service agency, offering a wide range of innovative programs designed to meet the multiple needs of people affected by AIDS in the Philadelphia area.

> **ActionAIDS**
> 1216 Arch Street
> Philadelphia, PA 19107
>
> **Pennsylvania's largest AIDS service organization, serving more than 2,500 men, women and children each year.**
>
> Contact:
>
> Kelly McBride or
> Harry A. Freedman
> Phone: (215) 981-3352

Demographic Analysis

Most of Dining Out for Life®'s 25,000 participants are included in the donor databases of the AIDS service organizations involved in the event. These individuals, who are committed to the cause and have substantial discretionary income, ask their friends and business associates to join them in dining out. The databases include more than 50,000 donors and volunteers in the tri-state area. Below is a summary of their demographic characteristics:

40% are mail order responders	41% have incomes greater than $51,000
82% are above the age of 36	65% own homes with values greater than $100,000
55% have lived in the same residence for more than 6 years	
47% are in the top 20% of the wealthiest people in America	
89% have credit cards	

Dining Out for Life® 1998
Participating Cities

Atlanta, GA	Baltimore, MD
Bloomsburg, PA	Boston, MA
Boulder, CO	Chicago, IL
Cleveland, OH	Columbus, OH
Cudahy, WI	Denver, CO
Indianapolis, IN	Knoxville, TN
Louisville, KY	Minneapolis, MN
Philadelphia, PA	Phoenix, AZ
Providence, RI	Safety Harbor, FL
San Francisco, CA	Seattle, WA
St. Louis, MO	Vancouver, BC
Washington, DC	West Hollywood, CA

To tap into this bounty, your group will have to make its request six months to a year in advance.

There are some good sources for this kind of information:

- Look up the names of companies on the Internet or at the library. Major corporate directories, such as Standard & Poor, provide a lot of information.

- If you are planning a large-scale search, the International Events Group compiles a sponsorship directory that contains the names of 1,800 top sponsors and what they fund. It comes on floppy disk and CD-ROM or on a rotating card file with cards.

- Other offerings available from IEG include indexes to various types of properties; who likes to donate to opera, fine arts, or car racing; how to find the most active sponsors in your market; and a free template that allows you to customize a proposal for sponsorship. The company also publishes a magazine that profiles companies and how they decide which causes to support.

While these tools are somewhat pricey, the newsletters alone can pay for themselves and can save the organization hours and hours of work, work that someone else has already done and updates yearly.

Other Creative Sponsorships

The Miami United Foundation for AIDS has worked out a program under which 40 restaurants donate 10% of the cost of each meal to the charity during a specified week. The charity gets the money and the donor participants get to experience a restaurant they may never have patronized before.

Whole Foods Market, a national chain of supermarkets, offers a 5% day once a month, during which 5% of all sales go to a specific charity. Each store has a team of people who decide which charities benefit.

The granddaddy of this kind of corporate involvement is Ben and Jerry's. The Vermont-based gourmet ice cream company will supply charities with a Ben and Jerry's ice cream stand or supply free ice cream. The money raised goes to the charity.

Many other large companies offer similar types of sponsorship. It is worth checking around to see if there are any you could get involved in. If not, con-

sider approaching a regional store to begin such a program, which would give it good community visibility.

Tapping into Money

For obtaining local money and support, consider an underwriting party. Draw up a list, like the one at the right, of the things you would like to have underwritten. Check your budget sheet to make sure you get them all.

Prior to the party, distribute the list of items and what each costs—these can be sent along with a letter of invitation that asks the recipients if they'd like to provide an item or make a cash donation to help underwrite the event. Then invite everyone to the underwriting party, which usually consists of cocktails and light refreshments. By drawing potential sponsors to your pre-event, you get them involved, and they might end up doing still more for the coming event.

At the party, announce the commitments you've already received and thank those companies for their participation. That's when you hand out the list of things yet to be underwritten, and when you encourage those who haven't yet done so to stand up and volunteer to help.

Some groups leave the underwriting chores to the events coordinator/manager or someone the coordinator/manager designates. Others use a committee to contact potential sponsors for support. Usually, the more business people on the committee, the more underwriting you'll get.

> **TIP** You can get a jump start on underwriting if you use networking. Bring together a committee that includes many influential, well-connected people who know the people in a position to provide significant underwriting.

One of the chairwomen of the Boca Raton, Florida, chapter of the American Red Cross formed a 30-member underwriting committee of influential people, all of whom had served as chairs for other prominent community agencies. Because every Floridian knows what horrors hurricanes can cause and how important the Red Cross is, it is possible to involve a broad base of community leaders. The goal of her affluent committee members: Secure underwriting for a ball to benefit the American Red Cross of the Palm Beaches.

SPECIAL EVENT
ITEMS FOR UNDERWRITING

ITEM(S)	GOAL

1-   **Advertising** $ _____

2-   **Awards and Plaques** $ _____

3-   **Dinner** $ _____
      Food & Service
      Liquor
      Wine & Champagne

4-   **Flowers and Decor** $ _____

5-   **Favors** $ _____

6-   **Music** $ _____
      Cocktail Party
      Dinner and Show

7-   **Printing** $ _____
      Invitations
      Tickets
      Press Packets
      Program Book
      Signage

8-   **Regular Cocktail Party** $ _____
      Food & Liquor
      Service

9-   **Photographers** $ _____

10- **Sound & Light Equipment** $ _____

11- **Party Design and Decoration** $ _____

12- **Transportation for Celebrities and VIP** $ _____
      Hotel Suites and Rooms
      Air Fare
      Limousines

The chairwoman hosted the committee for lunch at a country club. She outlined the budget for the event and prioritized the items that needed underwriting. She scheduled another meeting for six weeks hence, and told the committee members that by that time, she'd need the names of those who were underwriting each portion of the event. Committee members clearly understood that either they were to obtain the underwriting from others or cover it themselves. At the next meeting, the committee members had gathered $90,000 in underwriting, leaving the Red Cross chapter to cover only about $20,000 in potential event expenses. And they hadn't even sold the first ticket yet!

What the Giver Gets

In order to achieve a big success, you must be specific about what you need and what you can offer the sponsor in return. This applies to underwriting parties and to approaching companies and individuals on a one-on-one basis.

Keep in mind that most companies offer their sponsorship to build their image over the long term. A 1996 study found that 93% of the companies polled said they spent money on "cause-related marketing" to "build deeper relationships with customers." Eighty-nine percent wanted to "enhance corporate image and reputation." At least half also were looking to increase sales.

Most companies respond best to the promise of advertising in magazines, newspapers, or on television and radio in return for participation. Companies that do a lot of sponsorship expect a three-for-one return on their underwriting sponsorship dollars. That means that if they give $10,000 toward underwriting the music, they expect $30,000-worth of radio and TV air time in which their company name is mentioned, and space in print advertisements in which their company name and/or logo appear.

Following Up

Once the money has been spent, the event is over, and everyone's recovered a bit, follow up by writing each sponsor a thank-you note. Also include a wrap-up that provides the following information:

- How many people attended.
- Copies of everything that appeared in print in which the sponsor's name was mentioned—

flyers, invitations, advertisements, tickets, program books.
- Photos of whatever promotional material was up at the event, such as banners, a display, or a booth (try to photograph these when there are a lot of people around them).
- Obtain an advertising schedule that shows how often public service announcements or advertisements of the event were broadcast.

Finally, if you can afford it, purchase a small display ad in the local newspaper and use it to thank all of your sponsors. If you hope to get something in the news portion of the local paper, the photo and news release should arrive the day after the event as early as possible. You can contact the newspaper in advance and ask news staff to cover the event, but plan on having your own photographer and someone to write a few paragraphs.

> **TIP** Several weeks after the event, contact your sponsors once more and ask if they would like to sponsor the event again the following year. Chances are, if they were happy with how things went, they will sign on again. Ask for a larger amount!

Conflicts of Interest

Sometimes there are conflicts between a charity's goals or beliefs and those of the corporations that want to underwrite an event. Some conflicts are obvious, such as a tobacco company sponsoring a lung association or cancer society event. Charities must be vigilant in checking for situations with the potential for such problems. Although the corporation's intentions may be sincere, if potential donors find the connection offensive, the company's participation may hinder fundraising rather than enhance it.

Such a potential problem arose in the planning of a golf tournament benefit for the Addictions Institute, a Miami Beach center that trains counselors to work with people with addiction-related problems. The event was sponsored by the Miami Beach Chamber of Commerce. An area beer distributor wanted to be a sponsor, and this offer put the charity organizers in a difficult spot. They realized it would be in bad taste to allow a beer company to be the major sponsor of an event that helps people who cannot handle alcohol.

When the charity's staff discussed the problem

When the sponsor gets significant exposure through a charitable event, it's money well spent.

EVENT SPONSORSHIP FORM

CATHERINE CONNELLY CHILDREN'S FOUNDATION

A GALA EVENING AT MAR-A-LAGO

I would like to help support the Catherine Connelly Children's Foundation at the following level:

_____ **TITLE (EVENT) SPONSOR**   ($50,000)

- Prime Name Identification
- Corporate Name and Logo included in all Advertising and Promotions
- 100 Public Service Announcements on Radio
- 50 Public Service Announcements on TV
- Logo and Name on Cover of Program Book
- (2) Full Page ad, (1) Inside Plus Back Cover
- Photo & Speaking Opportunity at Pre-Event Reception
- Ringside Seating at Concert for 20 Guests
- Possible Distribution of Promotional Items

_____ CORPORATE AND INDIVIDUAL SPONSOR ($15,000 - $25,000)

- Name and/or Logo included in all Advertising and Promotions
- Public Service Announcements on Radio and TV
- 1 Full Gold Page Ad in Program Book
- Photo Opportunity at Event
- 16 Inner Circle Tickets at Sponsored Events

_____ BENEFACTOR   ($5,000 - $10,000)

- Name and/or Logo included in all Advertising and Promotions
- 1 Full Silver Page Ad in Program Book
- 10 tickets to Sponsored Events

Enclosed, please find my check in the following amount _____

Name_____

Company   Name_____

Address_____

         _____

City_____ST_____ZIP_____

Phone_____Fax_____

Please send checks to: The Catherine Connelly Children's Foundation with the Budweiser beer distributor officials, the beer people suggested that the charity approach Hooters, a popular beer-and-chicken-wings chain. The restaurant agreed to be a major sponsor and the event became the "Hooters Superweek Golf Tournament." The restaurant donated money, food, and advertising, and also hosted several preview events. The beer was sold at the event, not given free, to the public. The Budweiser distributor served as a minor sponsor, donating beverages (beer and soft drinks) that were provided along with dinner to the golfers. In exchange for its donation, the distributor's name appeared on the backs of golf carts and in the program while Hooters was more prominently featured in banners and promotional material for the event.

In May 1996, the San Diego Museum of Art sought underwriting for an upcoming exhibit. There were discussions with Philip Morris, the cigarette manufacturer, that caused significant protests from anti-tobacco activists, including the American Lung Association. Philip Morris did not underwrite the show.

Even if a particular sponsor doesn't fit with the event you're planning now, if the problem is handled with sensitivity, chances are you can involve that would-be sponsor in another, later event that would be more appropriate.

Chapter 4 Checklist

❏ Before you commit to hosting an event, seek sponsorship from area businesses and prominent individuals. Don't forget those who belong to your organization.

❏ Make a list of what needs underwriting and what each item costs.

❏ If you plan to hold an underwriting party, send the underwriting "wish list" along with the invitations. Ask potential underwriters to make a contribution.

❏ At the party, thank each sponsor who has already pledged support. Distribute a list of what remains to be underwritten, encouraging those who haven't committed to get involved.

❏ If possible, get a media sponsor—newspaper, magazine, radio, or television. Once you have the assurance of public exposure, more companies are apt to sign on.

❏ Be prepared to tell potential sponsors what they will get in return for their support—media advertising, a banner or booth at the event, the corporate name on all publicity sent out, etc.

❏ Immediately after the event, follow up with sponsors by writing each one a thank-you note. Let each sponsor know how many people attended the event. Send copies of any posters, ads, photos of banners or booths, plus a rundown on how many times commercials or PSAs played on radio or television.

❏ For events aimed at crowds of 2,500 or more, consider seeking underwriting from national companies. The cost of buying the IEG sponsor guides will allow you to start soliciting for help weeks earlier than if you'd had to search out all the information these books and reports contain.

❏ Consider other avenues of underwriting. Seek out several restaurants or food stores to donate a percentage of their sales to your organization.

❏ Be aware that in your eagerness to raise money, you might fail to recognize the conflicts of interest that could arise, such as a tobacco company supporting a heart or lung fundraiser. Try to involve such sponsors, but in a less public way, if possible.

Question: What's a camel?
Answer: A horse created by a committee.

While this is an old joke, there's a reason for its longevity: Left to their own devices, committees can run amuck.

Every event needs a well-organized working committee made up of motivated individuals who can make the event happen. There have been many disastrous events that featured star-studded honorary committees that may have lent an air of sophistication and allure, but the stars didn't get out there and sell tickets.

chapter 5

COMMITTEES AND COMMITMENTS

Think of committees in fishing terms: The honorary committee is the tasty bait; the working committee is the rod, reel, and hook. Organized and supervised properly, it's a winning combination, especially when the honorary chairpeople are encouraged to take an active role.

Miami's Community Alliance Against AIDS used the star-studded committee strategy successfully when it sponsored "An Extraordinary Evening with Elizabeth Taylor." Since the group was able to bill it as a night with Elizabeth Taylor, there were more people begging to be honorary committee members than were needed. There were 20 honorary chairpeople chosen, each of whom committed to host and underwrite all costs of a dinner at their home or a private club. They were given specific instructions: Not only were they to host dinners at their own expense, they were then to transport their group to the hotel for the show. Each chairman was assigned a celebrity who would be a guest at his or her dinner. Some of the stars who participated were Tommy Tune, Manhattan Transfer, Julio Iglesias, Zsa Zsa Gabor, Eddie Albert, Donna Summer, Petula Clark, and Donald O'Connor. Following the dessert and a show, Elizabeth Taylor addressed the gathering and presented an award. Some 1,200 people attended, and the event grossed $2.2 million.

In this example, the honorary committee played a much more active role than is usually the case. But even so, there were many people on working committees who made sure each of the 20 dinner parties and the grand finale at the Fontainebleau Hilton on Miami Beach went smoothly.

When you organize your team, every committee person should be invited via an individual letter to serve on that committee. The letter should clearly state the recipient's responsibilities: "As a member of the committee, you are expected to put together a table of ten friends," or "purchase ten tickets" or "acquire and install all decorations" or whatever. Other duties should also be clearly spelled out. The major role of a working committee—and, when possible, the honorary committee as well—is to sell (and perhaps also buy) tickets to your event.

Each committee should function as a cohesive group with two purposes: making the event a financial success and creating something enjoyable that people will want to attend again. This is often a hard balance to obtain. The key to keeping that balance is to have an event coordinator/manager who keeps track of all the tasks of committee members, someone who keeps an eye on the big picture (as explained in Chapter 3, Management).

For a dinner, for example, each committee member commits to buying one table and selling another one. If the group plans a 300-person event, each of 15 committee members buys a ten-seat table and sells another table for ten. The event quickly sells out. Even if a few people don't honor their commitments, the group has only a handful of tickets left to sell.

Getting People Involved

Adequate staffing is one of the keys to a successful outcome. Assess your board, paid staff, and key volunteers. Then figure out where you have gaps and go after the people you need to do those jobs.

Consider the case of Alicia Soames Petry (not her real name), a prominent South Florida socialite, who wanted to hold a big event at her lavish home to raise money for a local health charity. When the event coordinator/manager contacted her, she informed him she had already sent hold-the-date cards to 2,000 of her "closest friends." When the event coordinator/manager asked who was on her committee, she said, "I don't need a committee. When I invite my friends, they come."

The site for the party held more than 500 people. Only 130 people attended. Obviously, all were friends of Mrs. Petry's. If she'd used a committee of corporate and business sponsors, this event might have been a success.

The moral: No one person can do it all.

A few ways to get top-notch people involved include:

- Reading the social columns of local newspapers to determine who the movers and shakers are, then seeking them out.
- Looking for involvement from upper-level management of large corporations or businesses.
- Looking for new businesses moving into the area that might want to draw attention to themselves. Sometimes the principals are willing to sign on.
- Asking key volunteers to bring in friends, business associates, and acquaintances.
- Looking at large service companies such as accounting and law firms, banks, and stock brokerages for potential committee people. These people have large client bases to which they may be able to sell tickets.
- Seeking involvement of other service organizations whose major goals are fundraising, such as: the Junior League, Kiwanis, Rotary, and Optimists. These groups are particularly useful in helping to distribute publicity and make follow-up phone calls.
- Checking high schools and area colleges (don't forget fraternities and sororities) that might have service groups that would work for you. This is a great way to get young people involved.

Honorary Committees

Honorary committees normally consist of socially

prominent individuals—business leaders, religious leaders, politicians, socialites, celebrities—through whose participation you can attract people to support your cause. Generally, the honorary chairperson's role is limited to lending his or her good name to your event. Honoring a prominent chairperson at the event encourages the honoree to invite business associates and friends to attend.

Many honorary chairpeople like to be seen in the company of celebrities. The National Parkinson Foundation frequently secured prominent chairpeople because of the involvement of Bob Hope. When someone like Hope, the king of charitable fundraisers, got involved, major corporate donors lined up to be honorees at the annual Parkinson events. In this case, they knew that Hope would present their award and that this event would be photographed and publicized—and that made it highly coveted.

Working Committees

Working committees do just what the name implies: they work closely with the group's paid staff to produce the event, making sure their committee works within its budget. These committees often include:

DECORATIONS
This group comes up with the "look" of the event, and deals with vendors or a party planner to create that look. Members take care of renting tables and chairs, if necessary, and obtaining door prizes. (If you want to give away a great many of these, there should be a separate committee for door prizes.) This group also handles the assembling and dispensing of any giveaway bags guests might receive. Every member sells tickets.

ENTERTAINMENT
This committee coordinates music or whatever entertainment is planned, working closely with the events manager to acquire appropriate talent with-

> **TIP** If possible, ask either an attorney who is familiar with entertainment contracts or a local entertainment promoter to serve on this committee. That person can be responsible for reviewing the nuts and bolts of the contract and rider for entertainment.

in the amount budgeted. The events coordinator/manager usually negotiates the contracts with entertainers. All committee members sell tickets.

TABLE OR TICKET SALES
Although all committee members are supposed to sell tickets, this group is primarily responsible for ensuring ticket sales. The more people you have on this committee, the greater your ticket sales are likely to be.

Members of this group usually commit to buying a certain number of tickets each and selling a matching number. They formulate the list of people to whom invitations or notices will be mailed, and they solicit block purchases from corporations and individuals. A subgroup, the phone committee, does the follow-up phone calls to get people signed up.

For a large-scale event, "people needs" are always a concern. To help spread your workers further, consider using a ticket service agency. (See Chapter 3, Management) As noted in Chapter 3, these services, which have massive mailing lists, often send out a monthly newsletter. They also have outlets in many places and will handle the sales for you. As long as the event will require the sale of at least 2,500 tickets, using a ticket service can be well worth the cost. It can also reduce the number of people you will need for your ticket sales committee and make bookkeeping simpler.

PUBLICITY
If your organization is large enough to have paid staff members, these people normally handle publicity. But in some cases, a small cadre of volunteers can handle writing press releases, research who to send them to, send them out, and make follow-up calls. The same person who sends out the releases should do the follow-up phone calls.

Make sure only one person works with each media outlet. Newspapers, TV, and radio news broadcasters get many calls, and staff are apt to become hostile if they wind up with several people calling about the same event.

On the day of the event, one or two members of this committee usually serve as media liaison. All members sell tickets.

INVITATIONS
This can be either a committee unto itself or a subgroup of the decorations committee. This group compiles the mailing list or provides invitations to

> **TIP** Make sure to appoint at least one computer-literate person to this group to get the message out via the Internet, e-mail, and computer bulletin boards.

those people who have their own lists but don't want to release them. The committee chairman needs to follow up to make sure everyone who is doing personal mailings gets them out, and that all the invitations are mailed in a timely manner.

Because some committee people are reluctant to release the addresses and phone numbers of those to whom they mail invitations, ask the chairpeople for copies of the names only so you can merge that with your master list and eliminate duplicates. Once all the envelopes have be addressed, arrange them alphabetically or by ZIP code and again check for duplicates. Do this before you put postage on the envelopes.

This committee also decides on the design, format, and content of the invitations; negotiates and coordinates with the graphic artist and printer; and proofreads the invitation before it is sent out. All members sell tickets.

FOOD

This committee develops the menu, based on the event's theme and budget. It coordinates with the hotel, caterer, or volunteers who will prepare the food.

If your volunteers are purchasing and preparing the food, this may be a subgroup of the food committee, called the food preparation committee.

Either someone from this committee or the event coordinator/manager actually negotiates the contract with the hotel or caterer. If additional kitchen equipment is needed, this group sees that it is ordered, delivered, and returned. All members sell tickets.

REGISTRATION AND CHECK-IN

Registration and the work of the committee in charge of it starts long before the day of the event. One person—the chairperson, secretary, or volunteer—should be in charge of keeping track of who is coming. Other members of this committee make sure the proper equipment—computers, tables, chairs, etc.—are at the registration site. They determine what to give people as they check in— a program, table assignment card, etc. They handle check-in on the day of the event. All members sell tickets.

Search for a computer-literate person for this committee, too, someone who can set up and train other members to use the computer software now available that significantly simplifies registration and seating. See Chapter 12, Tools of the Trade, for a list of computer resources.

Set up a registration system. It can be a computerized list or something as simple as a shoe box with index cards inside. If you use a computer, have someone keep a detailed, running alphabetical list of who plans to attend. On this same list, you can also indicate whether the person has paid.

For example, if you're having a sit-down dinner, then every name should have a table number listed with it. You can also make a list with the number of tables you plan and eight spaces for each table. Fill in the names of those who will sit at each table. And for each person attending the dinner, the entry should list who they wish to sit with and their food preferences.

While the actual registration is done by staff or volunteers, the seating plan is formed by the chairperson and a few others. First, they should walk the room and decide how the tables will be set up. (Or, in the case of an outdoor crafts show, someone must decide the lineup of vendors the same way.)

Although many of your registration team may be experienced at it, it never hurts to practice before the guests arrive. If you have time, conduct a run-through at the event site. If that's not logistically possible, gather everyone for a practice session at someone's home or at your office a few days before the event. Assign some workers to play the parts of impatient guests, or those with registration problems. Teach the staff how to handle these situations. Also teach workers how to tactfully ask for money from those who have not paid. They should politely ask for a check or credit card (if you are accepting them) and, if the guest has neither, ask the guest to sign a pledge slip to pay later.

Consider renting beepers or portable phones for your key staff and registration desk. These devices make communication a lot easier (with one another as well as the vendor who hasn't shown up on time). If a problem arises, you can easily be reached on a portable phone. These are particularly handy in large outdoor facilities. If your budget can handle it, it's a good investment.

PROGRAM BOOK

This group decides how many pages the book will be and what it will look like. Members sell ads in the book, write whatever copy is needed, supervise printing, collect money from advertisers, and make sure the book gets distributed. This committee should be large. As with tickets, the more people involved, the more ads you will sell. All members sell tickets.

SPECIAL COMMITTEES

Many events require additional committees. For example, an auction must have an acquisitions committee. An arts and crafts or antique show calls for a committee to coordinate the vendors and booths. Consult your checklist to see if there are duties on it that do not fit into any of the above committees, then form the special committees needed to attend to them.

Depending on the size of your volunteer staff and the nature of the event, you may need as few as two committees or as many as ten.

A member of the working committee should meet regularly with members of honorary committees. Though this is time-consuming, it is time worth investing to make the event more successful. Regular contact allows the working committee repeated access to honorary committee members' contacts, i.e., the people with the most money. The more people you can approach to buy tickets or underwrite costs, the more money the group makes.

For example: Suppose a businessman on the honorary committee has just concluded a big deal with a client. When a working committee member talks with him, the businessman might suggest that his client be contacted to support the cause.

Honorary committee members generally are upper-income people with significant social prominence, while working committee members are apt to come from a broader spectrum of the economic scale.

Follow these guidelines to make sure working committees are consistently productive:

- The overall chair or staff person who supervises the running of the show divides the duties of an event among the committees and makes sure that each committee knows exactly what is expected.
- The overall supervisor designates the chair of each committee in writing, spelling out duties,

goals, and budgets. Pick chairs who are tactful, organized, and able to hold productive, concise meetings. They must also be willing to finish tasks that their committee members fail to complete.

- Meetings are necessary. However, do not meet simply for the sake of meeting. There should be a purpose to each gathering. Meetings should start and end on time, and they should be no more than an hour long. Thank all committee members at every meeting. When possible, take care of small matters by phone or fax. Since most people's time is at a premium, committees should gather only to report on progress and decide what is to be done next.

It's important to make sure all committees are under the direction of a single events or staff coordinator. As noted at the beginning of the chapter, committees left to their own devices can create big problems and they can quite possibly bring about financial disaster, too. Therefore, you must make it absolutely clear to all committee chairpeople that the charity's authorized representative is the only one permitted to make financial commitments.

A case in point: At a Miami Grand Prix Gala dinner for 600, the event planner was surprised to find that the menu had been changed from the agreed-upon chicken dish to a lobster-and-steak dinner. Obviously, there was a big difference in price. The chairperson of the food committee said a local supermarket chain had offered to donate the filet mignons and so the chairperson felt the group could afford the change. However, she failed to note that the addition of the lobster increased expenses by $6 per person, a total of $3,600.

> **TIP** Make sure all vendors know who in your group is authorized to make financial commitments for the event.

Committee Chairpeople's Responsibilities

The committee chairpeople should meet at least twice the month before the event so everyone has an overview of what is happening and can share ideas. All committee chairs should report monthly to the event coordinator. All committee chairs should also be responsible for submitting written estimates to the event coordinator/manager and for obtaining final approvals from that person before committing to the service provider.

Committees themselves should meet regularly: at least monthly up to six weeks prior to the event, then at least weekly.

> **TIP** By six weeks before the event, the committee chairpeople should create a detailed final list of what needs to be done before the event, who will do it, and when it must be completed.

The Relief Team

Events are very labor-intensive. In the few months before an event, it is helpful to have volunteers staffing the phones, helping with extra typing, stuffing envelopes and media packets, and helping to clean up loose ends. If you have in-house staff members, they should be responsible for everyday typing and correspondence, and other tasks related to day-to-day operations. Meanwhile, the event manager makes sure the event is proceeding on track operationally and financially.

The Event Coordinator/Manager's Role

The event coordinator keeps track of what each committee does and spends. He or she makes sure each committee is completing tasks on time and keeps the heads of the organization (board members or executive director) up to date on what's happening on all fronts. The event coordinator should also retrieve mailing lists from all committee people so they can be merged for invitation mailing, which should take place six weeks before the event. The coordinator should also organize committee members to write personal notes to key potential purchasers of blocks of tickets or tables.

The Consultant's Role

A consultant might work as part of the team, take on the role of the event manager, or simply advise. Usually consultants give advice, but don't actually handle the event.

Sometimes a consultant can help trim expenses, come up with additional ideas for generating revenue, and provide expertise the organization's staff might not have. A consultant's toughest job is to assess the likely outcome of an event, and if it appears that the event may be a failure, to advise that it be called off.

The Final All-out Effort

Three weeks before the event, gather as many volunteers as you can muster and stage an organized telephone follow-up. They should call everyone who received an invitation but has not yet responded. Try an appeal such as, "I'm calling for Mrs. Jones-Smythe. She's already purchased ten tickets to this event and she hopes you'll be able to join her. May I also put you down for a table near hers?"

> **TIP** By having people work the phone during the last three weeks, you can often double the number of people who attend. Here's where people power really counts.

Egos

Often, events fail because of egos. Too many people insist on having things their way, and they do so at the expense of the charity. In creating a fundraiser, it is important that the event coordinator/manager take a strong role so that your event doesn't turn into an out-of-control spending spree or clash of personalities.

First-class events can be run without $40,000 in flowers, European china, and free entry for dozens of good friends. It is far better to have raised $50,000 than for an event to break even—or lose money—after six months of hard work by hundreds of people. Everyone needs to feel important, but it is the role of the event coordinator/manager or the executive director to make the tough decisions and stick by them.

Thank-Yous and Recognition

Your major volunteers should always be listed on invitations, programs, and, if possible, in some sort of thank-you article in your organization newsletter or community newspaper. Remember to thank them briefly but publicly at the event as well. Special touches go a long way toward garnering loyalty.

Send every volunteer a note of appreciation and

A good event coordinator keeps everyone on-board, up-to-date, and on task.

Papanicolaou Woman's Corps
for Cancer Research, Inc.

Harry A Freedman
Executive Director

FAX MEMORANDUM

TO: Celia Lipton Farris

FROM: Harry Freedman

DATE: February 22, 1995

RE: **WOMEN WHO LEAD '95**
           CHECK LIST

Enclosed please find a working checklist of things that need to be accomplished prior to the Women Who Lead luncheon at The Breakers on March 9th. We can deal with most of this after your Sunday event at Mar-A-Lago.

It's great news that Shannon Donnelly will be doing an article about Mrs. Hope which we can follow with our full-page ad. A final proof of the ad should come to you some time this afternoon.

We will change the message on our recording to include a direct number to talk to a "real person", as well as the changes in prices. We will include all the honorees (Phyllis, Dolores, and Sally).

I have also sent you some initial information from the Breakers in reference to table arrangements and other details including a tentative menu.

I WILL CALL YOU LATER THIS AFTERNOON AFTER 3 P.M.

THANK YOU FOR BEING AN EXCELLENT ADVISOR AND GOOD FRIEND!!!

HAF

Regional Office • The Hallmark Building • 3800 South Ocean Drive • Suite 242 • Hollywood FL 33019 • (305) 454-8375 • Fax (305) 454-9858

The Papanicolaou Woman's Corps has been supporting cancer research since 1952

perhaps a small flowering plant. Or hold a modest thank-you luncheon. This will show volunteers that you appreciate their time, creativity and, most of all, their support.

Thank committee chairpeople with a certificate or plaque, if possible, along with an appropriate cover letter. These tokens of appreciation should be presented at the event so the recipients get public recognition for their work.

If you have gone over your goal or raised a substantial amount of money, this should be announced as part of the recognition of your volunteers' work. If there is a suitable place in your organization's headquarters or office, displaying plaques listing volunteers whose work made your event a success is a nice touch.

The Voluntary Action Center of the United Way of Central Indiana found a unique way to express gratitude. During National Volunteer Week, which is observed in late April, it organizes 50 callers to phone some 3,000 volunteers to thank them for their work that year. The center contacts local companies, who supply volunteer callers. Local notables—the mayor, sheriff, and others—are also asked to participate. Two companies donate the use of their headquarters for calling sites, and provide food and phones for the volunteers. Area groups prepare a list of those they wish to thank and the Thank-a-Thon phone team does the rest.

For individuals who performed over and above the call of duty or who raised substantial dollars individually, you might want to send flowers or a gift basket at your own expense. This attention to detail always pays off when you need to ask that special favor or to work hard again on the next event.

Photography

Send photographs from the event for publication in community newspapers. Photographs should also be sent to key committee people as another form of thanks, and as a remembrance.

Chapter 5 Checklist

❏ Assess your personnel resources. Then figure out how many more people you will need, encouraging those already on board to get others involved.

❏ Organize your honorary committee, confirming each person's involvement and responsibilities in writing.

❏ Organize working committees, confirming each person's involvement and responsibilities in writing.

❏ Have working committees meet once a month until six weeks before an event, then have them meet briefly every week.

❏ Chairpeople of each committee should meet with the event coordinator/manager at least once a month up to six weeks before an event, then weekly.

❏ Run through the registration procedures with workers before the event.

❏ Secure volunteers to help with last-minute tasks.

❏ Make sure there are enough people to handle follow-up phone calls in the last weeks before the event.

❏ Remember to thank all committee members at every meeting and to follow up after the event with a thank-you note, plaque, photos, or small gift.

chapter **6**

LOCATIONS, LOCATIONS, LOCATIONS

It may be that cousin Courtney had a lovely wedding at that perfectly restored historic home in the park. And the Katz bar mitzvah was a smash hit in the circus tent at the fairgrounds. But in neither case was budget a primary consideration when these well-to-do families planned their children's celebrations.

For a nonprofit group, usefulness, not beauty, is a far better measurement of a site's suitability. It is much less expensive to decorate a plain room than it is to truck in kitchen equipment, tables, and toilets to a spectacular site.

When the University of Miami's Sylvester Comprehensive Cancer Center held an event, the group began with an unadorned courtyard on the Center's grounds. The decorating committee transformed it into a glamorous nighttime setting by building a stage in front of a building with columns that made it seem like a stage set. The stage projected out from the steps leading to the building. Trees throughout the courtyard twinkled with small white lights. Because of good planning and imagination, this group created a perfect under-the-stars setting from an ordinary spot and on a limited budget.

Researching the Right Site

When discussing a site, many of your committee people will suggest places based on their experiences there. But in most cases, those experiences began after the site was fixed up. People generally have no idea of how much time and money it takes to make a place look the way it does and function the way it is supposed to.

That's why it is up to the event coordinator/manager and chairperson to do the research required to make a practical location choice, rather than acceding to committee members' enthusiasm for a beautiful, but possibly unsuitable, site. That means you need not—and should not—look for the biggest, flashiest, most expensive spot you can find. Instead, seek out one that can provide you with the basics at a price that is within your budget and leaves sufficient funds for decorating. Of course, the best of all possibilities is to find a site that meets all the practical needs of the event and also has some aesthetic appeal.

It may seem like a monumental task to determine which site will be best, but a systematic approach helps streamline the process.

Site Factors to Consider

There are four basic site factors to consider: location, cost, size, and facilities that are available at the site. Consider each factor and figure out how it applies to your event and the places you consider.

First, develop a list of possible locations. Look in magazines and newspapers, such as *People, In Style,* and *Town & Country,* and upscale local magazines and local newspapers for articles on social events held at unusual party sites.

Another place to look is in the "Yellow Pages" under churches, halls, caterers, hotels, restaurants, parks and historic sites, and recreation. With some creativity, a farm field, park, or gigantic parking lot can hold top-notch events. In colder climates, consider ice skating rinks and ski resorts. In warmer regions, consider public beaches. Establish a file of sites for future reference.

Another good source of inspiration is *The Fundraising Formula, 50 Creative Events Proven Successful Nationwide,* by Katie Kraatz and Julie Haynes (Taft, 1987).

One group that uses out-of-the-ordinary sites to great advantage is The Foundation for Architecture in Philadelphia. More than 4,000 people attend the group's annual Beaux Arts Ball. The ball is held around Halloween in buildings that are either under construction or in the process of renovation. The organization uses the money it raises to fund the preservation of historic buildings.

The group has used such sites as the elegant, historic, and now-defunct downtown department store, Wanamaker's. The affair took place on the spacious top two floors of the store, which had been gutted in preparation for renovation. The developer, eager for a chance to bring in thousands of people, paid the foundation to hold the event there, and the foundation used that money to market the ball. The plumbing and electrical contractors working on the renovation installed toilets and did the necessary electrical work, donating about $90,000 in goods and services.

Other than the basic electricity and some construction lighting, there was nothing but a vast open space with which to work. The Foundation added lights, created a haunted house area, a section for refreshments, and a big stage for the costume parade, plus dance areas with different types of music in each. There were huge platforms on which costumed guests could display their outfits, and closed-circuit television sets so guests in one area could see what was happening elsewhere. The group served dinner to 1,000 people on the eleventh floor, then hosted some 4,000 people at the ball and costume parade on the twelfth floor.

The ball grossed $525,000, netting $262,000, about a 50% return. This was not only a fundraiser, it was a friend-raiser, because it exposed thousands of people to the group and its work.

While this event works well for the Architecture Foundation, such a lavish event won't work for every group. This is the kind of event that could ruin less financially secure groups. The Beaux Arts Ball has grown over the years. It's built up a following, and has a generous supply of front money.

But the lesson here is not to limit yourself to places you would categorize as banquet facilities—there are all sorts of places capable of handling events that you may have overlooked.

Take the humble field, for example, the perfect spot for cow-chip bingo, which requires only the field and a just-fed bovine. Simply mark off squares on the field, sell each one for a set amount, then place the cow on it and let the chips fall where they may. The owner of the piece of field that the cow graces by dropping her chips is the winner. This event needs little setup or up-front financial outlay, requires few committee members, and can raise $25,000 to $75,000.

A few lesser-known, but possibly suitable, locations might include airplane hangars, public gardens, lighthouses, museums, plantations, parks, stadiums, boats, shopping centers, country clubs, schools, and wineries. Consider renting out a whole restaurant—or a bare banquet room—and create a theme if you can't find an appropriate theme in place anywhere. Unusual sites will vary from city to city, but what works elsewhere might well be adapted to your town.

Share Our Strength (SOS) Taste of the Nation parties through the country combine an eclectic mix of food, wine, and spirits from leading city chefs, restaurants, beverage companies, and food suppliers. American Express covers the basic costs and print and advertising, so these events are sure moneymakers that attract new friends to support hunger relief. The parties are fun, everyone gets to sample interesting food and socialize, and the restaurants have the opportunity to introduce themselves to potential customers. But your gathering needn't be in a restaurant; you can hold it almost anyplace.

Charities can raise large amounts because the restaurants donate food and staff, large corporations might cover invitations and publicity in the media, and hotels and other facilities often donate the site. Tie in an auction of coupons for dinners at participating restaurants, drinks, and other packages. Added to the entry fee guests pay, this is a very lucrative event.

Another option is to offer a place where most people ordinarily aren't admitted. Special-location gatherings can raise lots of money for your charity if they are held in a spectacular home, a unique corporate setting, or other unusual location, and chaired by high-powered but often inaccessible executives.

For example, David Geffen, one of the partners in the entertainment triumvirate DreamWorks, hosted a series of intimate dinners to raise funds for the 1996 re-election of President Clinton. Attendees paid $50,000 to $100,000 to attend these soirées with fellow movers and shakers from the entertainment field. These gatherings raised millions, using only a few strategic phone calls and power networking.

Once you have a list of possible locations, begin to fill out a location survey form for each. Contact each establishment by phone to get as much of the survey information as possible. Compare the surveys and strike from the list any sites that are too small, too large, too expensive, or too booked up.

Once you have narrowed your choices down to two or three possibilities, ask the establishment's manager for the names and telephone numbers of other organizations that have held affairs there. Contact someone from each group to find out how the events turned out, how well the site met their needs, and what shortcomings or strengths they discovered.

Or consider one location for which you can forget about budgets, planning menus, and worrying about kitchen capabilities. Celebrities Cruise for Charity, developed by The Cruise Lines, Inc., helps large charities with members who like to cruise. It is ideal for an organization with ten or more chapters and a mailing list of 3,500 or more contributors who contribute an average of $500.

Celebrities Cruise for Charity offers fundraising experts who help maximize your fundraising through additional on-board events. Besides the cruise, celebrities are available to large-enough cruise groups. For each berth a participant reserves, the charity gets $100. The more berths the charity sells, the more free berths it earns, and it can then sell these additional rooms for more profit. All items such as food, decorations, flowers, and such are included in the price of the cruise. (See the cost comparison between sponsoring a celebrity cruise and hosting a dinner gala on page 14.)

Ordinarily, people will drive to the event. When considering a site, think about how easy the place is to find. If it is an evening event, will people feel safe driving there at night? Is there adequate parking close to the building?

Sometimes the location is fixed and you have to work around it. Such was the case when the new Kenneth Cole shoe store opened in the high-fashion district of Miami Beach's chic South Beach. The three-story store held a maximum of 150 people, but between 700 and 900 guests were expected. So the event coordinator got a permit to close the street in front of the store and tented half the street. People could walk in and out of the tent, wander into the store, sample hors d'oeuvres, and mingle with celebrities such as Madonna, Kenneth Cole, and Calvin Klein.

During the opening party and all the following week, the store donated 10% of its sales to support Health Crisis Network, an AIDS service organization in Miami. The clever invitation read: "You might

LOCATION SURVEY

1. Name of site _____

2. Address _____

3. Phone and contact person_____

4. Ownership (public or private) _____

5. Dimensions of space to be used_____

6. Indoor or outdoor _____

7. If indoor, is it air conditioned/heated? _____

8. What sort of bathroom facilities are available? _____

9. How many people will it hold? _____

10. Parking (valet or self-parking, how many spots?)_____

11. Dates available _____

12. Cost_____

13. What's included in the rental cost? _____

14. What will cost extra? (for example, renting tents, chairs, portable stages) _____

    _____

15. Restrictions or permits needed. _____

    _____

16. Are adequate electric outlets and systems available?_____

17. Is audiovisual equipment available? _____

18. Is kitchen equipment available? _____

19. Deposit: How much? When due? _____

20. Refund/cancellation policy. _____

21. Is there on-site custodian/security? _____

22. Is storage space available? Can it be secured? Cost? _____

23. Fire standards? Is fire insurance included in price? _____

24. Is there liability insurance? _____

25. Can you bring in the caterer of your choice or is there an approved list? (Hotels, of course, will not allow outside caterers.) _____

    _____

An event order for a site should clearly state what the location will provide, when, where, for how many, and at what cost.

```
EO# 000030292              EVENT ORDER           DATE: THU. MAR  9,1995
------------------------------------------------------------------------
FUNCTION: PAPANICOLAOU CANCER RESEARCH      TYPE : RECEPTION
POST AS :                                    MGR  KATHRYN C. MURRAY
CONTACT : MR. HARRY FREEDMAN               PHONE: 305-454-8375
          3800 South Ocean Drive
          Suite 242
          Hollywood, Fl 33019
                                                  ACCOUNT: 3032095
BILLING : SOCIAL
------------------------------------------------------------------------
    TIME              ROOM                     GUARANTEE     SET
 11:00 A - 11:45    FLORENTINE D/R               350        400
------------------------------------------------------------------------

FOOD:
  Hors D'Oeuvres to be passed - Type to be advised

BEVERAGE:
  TO BE PASSED AS GUESTS ENTER
      .
  Mimosas                                    6.00  Each
  White Wine                                24.00  P/BOTTLE
  Bloody Marys                               4.75  EACH
  Assorted Fruit Juices - (Orange, Cranberry, Apple)   2.25  EACH
  Perrier with Lime                          2.75  EACH

SET UP:
  2 Registration Tables outside Room with Lamps
  15 Cocktail Tables with Chairs
  1 Raffle Table
  Raffle Drum Needed

LINEN:
  Linen Color to be advised                  1.50  P/Person

MISCELLANEOUS:
  Photographer - Lucien Capart

SPECIAL NOTES:
  Vallet Parking
------------------------------------------------------------------------




  All food & beverage prices are subject to 19% service charge & 6% tax.

  A guarantee figure must be given 48 hours prior to the function.  If
  the count is not received at that time, THE BREAKERS will use the
  estimated figure as the final guarantee.

  Arrangements Accepted By: _____
```

```
EO# 000030293              EVENT ORDER            DATE: THU. MAR  9,1995
-------------------------------------------------------------------------
FUNCTION: PAPANICOLAOU CANCER RESEARCH      TYPE : LUNCH
POST AS :                                   MGR  KATHRYN C. MURRAY
CONTACT : MR. HARRY FREEDMAN                PHONE: 305-454-8375
          3800 South Ocean Drive
          Suite 242
          Hollywood, Fl 33019
BILLING : SOCIAL                                 ACCOUNT: 3032095
-------------------------------------------------------------------------
    TIME            ROOM                          GUARANTEE    SET
11:45. A -  3:00 P VENETIAN                          350       400
-------------------------------------------------------------------------

FOOD:
 Florida Citrus Salad with Assorted Field Greens      22.00  P/Person
 Raspberry Vinaigrette Dressing to be passed

 Chicken Wellington - Sauce Supreme
 With Julienne of Fresh Vegetables
 White and Wild Rice

 Luncheon Rolls to include, Wheat Rolls, Lavosh
 Sour dough and Cheese Bisquits

 Laced Doily
 With Chocolate Base
 Filled with Tri-Color Sorbets
 (Lemon, Mango and Raspberry)
 Fresh Berries and Coulis on plate

 Freshly Brewed Regular, Decaffeinated and Selection of Teas
 Iced Tea

BEVERAGE:
 Wine with Lunch To Be Advised

SET UP:
 Floor plan to be provided
 72" Rounds of 10 and 12
 2 Registration Tables outide of Venetian
 Head Table for 8 on Riser East Wall

LINEN:
 Linen color to be advised

AUDIO VISUAL:
 Table Top Podium and Mike
-------------------------------------------------------------------------
   All food & beverage prices are subject to 19% service charge & 6% tax.

   A guarantee figure must be given 48 hours prior to the function.  If
   the count is not received at that time, THE BREAKERS will use the
   estimated figure as the final guarantee.

   Arrangements Accepted By: _____
```

```
EO# 000030293              EVENT ORDER          DATE: THU. MAR  9,1995
------------------------------------------------------------------------
FUNCTION: PAPANICOLAOU CANCER RESEARCH      TYPE : LUNCH
POST AS :                                   MGR   KATHRYN C. MURRAY
CONTACT : MR. HARRY FREEDMAN                PHONE: 305-454-8375
          3800 South Ocean Drive
          Suite 242
          Hollywood, Fl 33019
BILLING : SOCIAL                                     ACCOUNT: 3032095
------------------------------------------------------------------------
     TIME              ROOM                          GUARANTEE    SET
  11:45 A -  3:00 P VENETIAN                            350       400
------------------------------------------------------------------------

     AUDIO VISUAL:
      Any Furter AV To Be Advised

     FLORAL/DECOR:
      Client To Provide

     MISCELLANEOUS:
      Photographer - Lucien Capart

     SPECIAL NOTES:
      Program will take place after lunch
      .
      Have Shades up for Lunch and Down for Speaker
------------------------------------------------------------------------
```

All food & beverage prices are subject to 19% service charge & 6% tax.

A guarantee figure must be given 48 hours prior to the function. If
the count is not received at that time, THE BREAKERS will use the
estimated figure as the final guarantee.

Arrangements Accepted By: _____

When drawing up a site plan, take into consideration room size, focal point, entrances, and traffic flow.

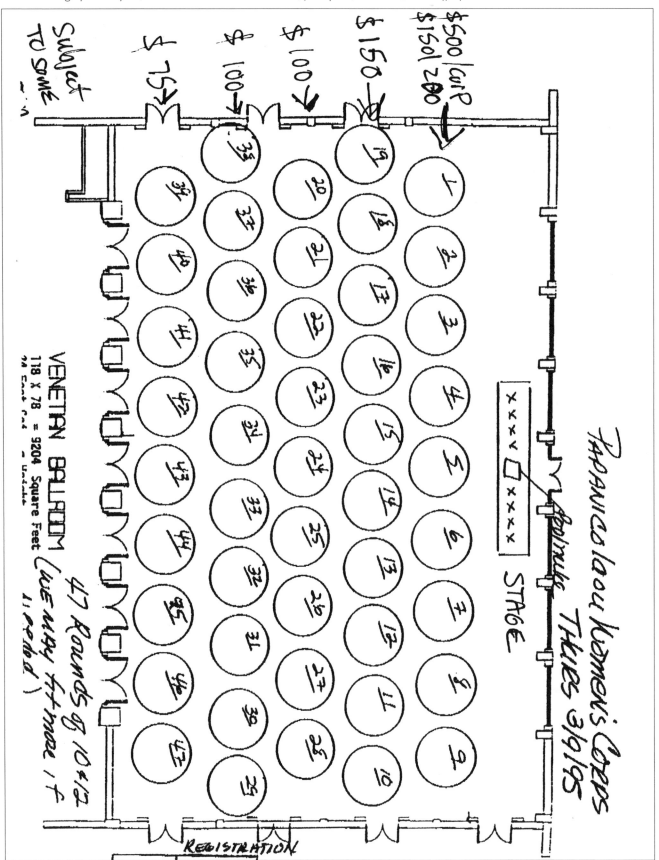

A good site plan will make assigning seats a cinch.

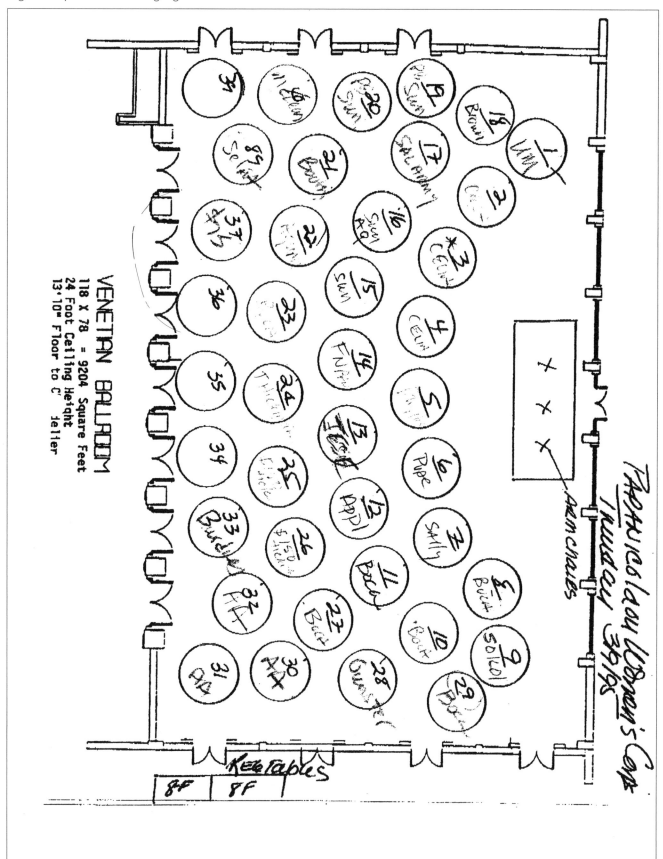

have to pull some strings to get into this party." Inside was a shoelace. Kenneth Cole Shoes paid for the entire event, so the Health Crisis Network got all the money raised.

Cost

How much can you afford to spend? (Refer to the budget worksheet on pages 24–26.) When figuring out the cost of a site, make sure you take into consideration what else you will need if you rent it. For example, you may find a lovely hall, but it might not have kitchen facilities, or bathrooms, or enough chairs and tables. If you have to rent these in addition to the room, the cost of using this site rises. This is especially true of outdoor sites. The base rental price will usually be lower than an indoor site, but you must rent many of the items that are included in the rental of a hotel ballroom or banquet hall, such as all the items mentioned above. Also, find out how much setup time you will be allowed. It can take several hours to prepare a room for an event (setting up tables, chairs, dishes, decor, and staging). Make sure you'll have access to the room in time and what (if any) additional costs might be involved.

TIP Find out who will be using the room before you and what decorations they will be using. If their decor fits with your plan, ask the previous occupant to donate the decorations to your group. That saves you the expense of buying and setting up more decorations, and the previous group saves time cleaning up.

When the University of Miami/Jackson Memorial Burn Center held an event, it saved a bundle by holding the affair in a room used the previous day for a convention dinner of the National Basketball Association. When asked, NBA officials readily agreed to donate the $20,000 in decor. In addition to the money saved by the Burn Center, no one from the committee had to spend time decorating.

For some events, such as fashion shows, you may need a full day to set up. In these cases, it may be necessary to reserve the room for the whole day. The establishment may charge extra for tying up the room that long, although some raise the price of the food instead.

Size

Room size is the trickiest part of site selection. The type of event you plan plays a major role in determining the size site you need. Considerably smaller space is needed to hold 200 people for a cocktail party than that required for a sit-down dinner for the same number. If the crowd just barely fit into the room last year and you are adding a fashion or stage show this time, you are going to need a larger space. When it comes to the fashion show, the runways can play havoc with your space.

 TIP How much room is enough? Here are the basic guidelines:
- For stand-up buffets and receptions, figure on 8 to 10 square feet per person.
- For a show in a theater or auditorium, plan on 10 to 12 square feet per person.
- For a seated banquet, you need about 12 square feet per person.
- If you plan dancing as well, add 2 square feet per person to the numbers above.
- For meals in tented events, don't forget to calculate space for the kitchen and prep tents.

Make a list of activities, then mentally walk through the event. Where will the registration table go? Where will people have cocktails? Where are they going to eat dinner? Where will the stage be? Where will the actors dress? Will there be a reception line? If so, where will it form?

Measure the site. Multiply the length by the width to get the total square footage. Subtract space for areas that block views or impede traffic.

Site Facilities

Picking a site can be like buying a dress or suit: At first glance, you may love the look of it so much that you overlook a less-than-perfect fit. But the first time you wear it in public, you notice all its flaws.

A site that looks good but doesn't have the facilities to fit your event can be a disaster. While you want it to be attractive, remember that your decorations committee can do much to beautify a less-than-perfect site. What you must have are basic necessities, such as adequate parking, enough space for the number of people expected to attend, sufficient kitchen and bathroom facilities, and staff.

In considering an outdoor site, remember that you can end up spending thousands of dollars bringing in things such as portable toilets, electricity, lights, sound equipment, flooring, air conditioning or heating, and maybe a tent. Then, after you have gone to the added expense, you are still dependent on the whims of nature to provide good weather. Such considerations are why more than two-thirds of all events take place in hotels, halls, auditoriums, theaters, or houses of worship.

For example, when the Florida South Chapter of the American Society of Interior Designers decided to hold a benefit, the committee dreamed up a Designers Weekend at an area racetrack. The committee envisioned a weekend-long event that would include tents in which designers would each create a room and setting. There would be a cocktail reception to kick off the event, races, food booths, a program book, and a dinner Saturday night under the tent with a celebrity entertainer.

TIP For outdoor sites, visit after a heavy rain to check for flooding. If you plan to erect a tent, make sure the ground will support the tent anchors. A floor, and heating or air conditioning, may be required. All of these greatly increase costs.

When the group drew up its initial budget, it totaled $292,500. This didn't include wine and liquor, which the committee hoped to have donated. The budget did, however, account for most of the anticipated expenses, including the rental of all the equipment that would have to be brought to the site.

The group expected to gross $465,500, which meant it would raise $173,000—not a great fundraising effort, even on paper. That assumed that 900 people would pay $250 to $500 each to have dinner under a tent at a racetrack. (Established events in the city charging a maximum of $250 often do not attract that many people.)

The other expense the committee didn't figure in was the cost of bringing in a star's staff and musicians. By the time everything was added up, it looked as if this was going to be a very time-con-

suming event—and a money-loser, too.

The main problem: The location didn't have adequate facilities for the type of activities the group planned.

When the event coordinator/manager contacted a local hotel catering director and found the director had had a cancellation on the date the group wanted, he booked the event into the hotel. Instead of tents, the huge second-floor atrium lobby of the hotel provided the perfect space for the cocktail reception, designers' areas, and food booths. Later, the adjacent ballroom was used for dinner for 700 people. A show followed dinner.

The event cost much less to stage in the hotel, and the charity made a profit of $25,000. Had it held to its original plan and site, the event probably would have lost a lot of money—all because of the cost of bringing in facilities.

Think about other facilities your event might need. Besides the primary site at which the event occurs, most events require additional space, such as a registration area, a place to prepare food and one to serve it from, and perhaps a place for a piano or musical trio to perform during cocktails. And then there are the general convenience factors: Where will the event be in relation to a coatroom and rest rooms? (At outdoor events, you generally have to bring in portable facilities.)

Setting Sites

After phoning the sites and checking their references, it should be easy to come up with the top three. Either the event coordinator/manager or chairperson or both should then inspect the sites, particularly the kitchen, ballroom, and parking. They should talk with the banquet manager to determine whether they feel comfortable working with him or her. They should ask the manager if the staff regularly works at the site or if the site hires staff on an as-needed basis from an agency. Results are generally better when the staff is consistent and familiar with the site.

Once you are sure of a site, arrange to get a copy of the site plan from the facility so you can map out how you're going to use the space. Most ballrooms have table plans that have been used successfully at previous buffets, fashion shows, and such. Ask for seating plans if they aren't forthcoming.

If you aren't working with a hotel and there isn't

> **TIP** For parking, figure on about half as many spaces as people you expect. There should be one valet per twenty-five cars.

a selection of room setups, you should draw up your own plan. First, create a site plan. Map entrances and exits, the light switches, the sound system controls, bathrooms, coatroom, first-aid area, trash dumpster, and parking. You should consider what events will take place and how traffic should flow. When possible, arrange to observe a similar event at the site before yours.

Doing a walk-through of your event in the empty room can help you determine what goes where.

Sometimes the location you choose just won't accommodate everything in one place. If you don't have one room big enough for everything, figure out a way to use several areas of the site at which you can arrange several small dining areas, with food set up in another spot, entertainment in yet a third. Once you know how you plan to use the space, make sure it is all spelled out in the contract—before you sign and before you pay a deposit and send out invitations.

Chapter 6 Checklist

- ❏ Develop a list of potential sites.
- ❏ Create a site survey form.
- ❏ Contact each site and collect information.
- ❏ Determine what permits may need to be obtained.
- ❏ Get three bids for rental items, such as tents.
- ❏ Ask for and check recommendations with groups that have used this site.
- ❏ Narrow the field to the top three choices.
- ❏ Visit each site.
- ❏ Check for its suitability in cost, size, facilities, and location.
- ❏ Map out how you plan to use the site.
- ❏ Make sure the site will work for your event.
- ❏ If it is an outdoor site, check into weather-interruption insurance and buy it if you can.
- ❏ Negotiate the contract. Stipulate everything in writing.
- ❏ Sign contract. Keep copies.

You've got a theme, a date, and a location. Now it's time to start selling. Word of mouth is the cheapest method, and can be quite effective. Ask your volunteers to talk up your event to people they know and recruit others to do so, too. Also ask your volunteers to develop a target list that reflects a cross-section of influential voices in the community. Those best able to spread the word are the people who come into contact with a lot of people, such as store owners, hairdressers, accountants, lawyers, stockbrokers, physicians, real estate agents, and anyone else with a large client base and who talks to a lot of people each day.

chapter 7

THE MESSAGE AND THE MEDIA

Media Promotion

A prime, but often overlooked, avenue for advertising is tying media promotion in with ticket sales. Try arranging a contest with a radio station, television station, or newspaper. If possible, line up all three. In exchange for a specified number of on-air spots or print ads promoting the event, the charity will give away a certain number of tickets as prizes. This creates repeated, large-scale exposure for the event and helps promote outside sales.

You can also buy advertising, just as any company does. Newspapers, magazines, and radio and television stations sometimes offer charities lower rates. Don't forget the smaller weekly papers. Many of these are distributed free, and so have great exposure along

Small but well-placed ads help boost media exposure.

with substantially lower ad rates. If you have a large corporate sponsor, that sponsor might be willing to buy commercial time or ad space for the charity in return for promoting the company's product at the same time.

When the University of Miami Burn Center held a scavenger hunt in downtown Miami, Florida, the *Miami Herald* donated $7,500 in advertising. The names of all the sponsors, including the *Herald*, were printed on the event T-shirts, displayed on banners in the refreshment area, and places along the hunt route. The *Herald* agreed to participate because it brought people into the downtown area and supported the Burn Center, while also giving the paper prime exposure.

 TIP   Ask companies that send out regular mailings or bills—banks, utilities, department stores—to let you include a statement stuffer. Don't forget in-house corporate newsletters. You provide the actual enclosures or a camera-ready copy according to the company's specifications. This is a good way to get broad publicity at very little cost.

Invitation Events

When invitations are sent out for an event, you should follow standard direct mail procedures. Mail the invitations early and, when possible, use first-class "address correction request" to clean up your mailing list. If mailing in bulk, follow post office procedure for separating by ZIP code.

TIP   By compiling your mailing list well in advance, you will know how many invitations you will need.

Good lists are the key to success. Your carefully selected chairpeople form committees, then everyone provides names, addresses, and phone numbers of all the affluent community people they know. Add to your master list the names of anyone who has previously contributed to your cause. If possible, acquire lists from other charities and organizations (or client lists from businesses). Merge all of these to ensure that no one gets multiple invitations. Check for duplicate mailings before affixing postage.

IDENTIFICATION

If you have an identifiable image, use it. Miami's Burn Center uses Snuffy, the dalmatian mascot for a talking fire truck used in the Burn Center's educational program. Fire fighting and dalmatians are a natural combination. The Burn Center used Snuffy's image for several events, dressing him appropriately for each one: For a beach party, he wore a Hawaiian shirt and sunglasses; for a scavenger hunt, he donned a Sherlock Holmes cape and pipe; for an auction, he wore a spiffy red bow tie and tuxedo. On the Burn Center's logo, the lettering is fire-engine red, and it's accompanied by the dalmatian. Thus, people came to associate the image and colors with the charity.

Besides a distinctive symbol, invitations should be eye-catching and well designed, and include:

- The name of the event
- The sponsoring organization
- The date and time
- The location
- The purpose and theme
- Committee and chairpeople
- Cost and to whom checks should be made out
- Deadline for response
- Honorees, if any
- What will be served (lunch, cocktails, etc.)
- Attire (formal or informal, other specifics as necessary)
- Board of directors (optional)
- Return envelope and reply card

TIP Arrange to have returns mailed to a prominent person in the community. You will get a better response if replies go to a well-known person instead of a faceless organization.

Invitations: The Whole "How-To"

MULTIPART INVITATIONS

Some invitations now come with several parts. For example, if an auction is part of the event, to lure people to the event and so they will be prepared to spend, list some of the best items available. To offer a variety of ways in which patrons can donate, you might want to enclose a raffle booklet so they can contribute even if they can't attend. Other, similar options in this vein are to include one or more

A successful reply card might give donors several options for ways to show support.

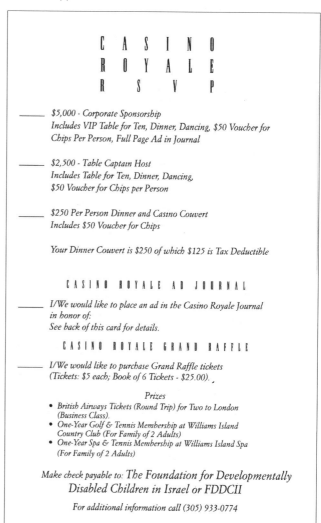

raffle tickets priced at about $25, a block of tickets for $100, or tickets to the event at $175 (or whatever you've decided to charge).

If you decide to add separate items, make sure you account for the additional postage in your budget. However, the added cost is apt to pay for itself, because it gives potential contributors choices as to how they wish to donate.

ADVANCE NOTICE

Don't forget to have save-the-date cards printed. These should be sent out well in advance of the event—at least six to eight weeks before the invitations go out.

Don't limit your advance notice to invitations.

Please join us for the

MULTI MILLION DOLLAR AUCTION
EXTRAVAGANZA
on Wednesday
December 13, 1995
6 pm
at
The Auto Toy Store Group
1624 E. Sunrise Blvd.
Fort Lauderdale, FL

★ *Starring* ★

Paintings, Bronzes, Sculptures

Designer Christian Llinares
exclusive fashion show from France

Fabulous Jewels by Mirabella

Exciting Travel Packages & Memorabilia

Exotic Automobile

with a host of celebrity auctioneers

UFA

To benefit United Foundation for AIDS
South Shore Hospital Community AIDS Program

Buffet and open bar
Attire: Holiday Chic

Come experience the spirit
of the Grand Prix Gala.

Dine from 7:30 P.M. to 9:30 P.M.
in our fabulous
International Dining Galleries.

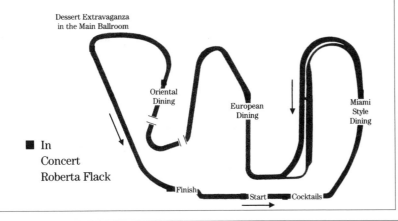

As noted elsewhere, credit-card companies, local utilities, department stores, and banks all send out monthly statements. Ask them if you can include a promotional insert in one of their billings. Also, travel bureaus and chambers of commerce often publish monthly or weekly newsletters through which you can get publicity, sometimes without charge.

And don't forget the high-tech methods. Use your computer to compose a letter, then fax it. Have Internet-connected members send e-mail to anyone they correspond with. If you have a website, feature the event prominently prior to the date. If you have the budget to do so and a large enough event to justify it, buy time on the Internet through one of the providers (America OnLine, Prodigy, or a local provider). If your event includes a celebrity appearance, buy three hours on the Internet to have your celebrity appear in a cyberspace chat room, talking with real people and helping to promote your cause.

A FRESH LOOK

What could possibly be new in the way of invitations? Lots! Innovative ones continue to pop up, such as one for the much-anticipated opening of the Astor Hotel on Miami Beach, Florida. Recipients opened the envelope and found a folder inviting them to the event and directing them to listen to the enclosed CD for details. When they played the CD, listeners got a "radio commercial" on the details. The "commercial" was followed by a mini-concert by Sister Sledge, the headliner at the opening, singing "We Are Family." (They also sang this on the night of the event.)

Another way to draw attention is to send out small stuffed animals with notes of invitation attached to their collars. These little furballs are eye-catching and can be less expensive than standard invitations.

ORDERING INVITATIONS

The first thing to determine is how many invitations you need (enough to cover your mailing list plus an additional 25% for publicity, extras to hand out, and a back-up supply).

Then figure out how many pieces will be in the invitation (outside envelope, inside envelope, invitation, reply card, return envelope, personal note card, raffle tickets, auction sampler, etc.).

Hire a graphic artist to design an appealing invitation. Make sure the artist understands postal regulations regarding size and weight. Discuss how many colors of ink and the kinds of paper you would like used. Discuss the design: How expensive do you want it to look? You don't want it to look as lavish as those often used for weddings or elaborate corporate events, or it will look as if you have spent too much money. The exception to this rule is when the cost of the invitations is totally underwritten and this is stated on the invitation.

With design in hand, you are ready to have your invitation printed. Ask around for reputable printers. Try to get at least three bids. Always check references, too, making sure to ask each customer if the printer not only delivered good-quality work, but did so on time. Find out if the printer will provide the invitation in pieces, providing envelopes first so addressing can begin. Since printers often have equipment to fold and collate your invitations, make sure to ask for it. It's a great time-saver.

When the printer gives you the invitation proof, have three or more people proofread it. Proofread carefully to make sure all the information is correct. Double-check the date, time, place, and the spelling of committee members' and sponsors' names. Also, find someone not involved in the project to look it over, too. This may sound silly or obvious, but all too often invitations go out lacking vital information such as the time or date, or containing the wrong information. While misspellings may seem trivial, they are actually extremely important. An error such as a misspelled name can cause hard feelings and might cost you a valuable volunteer or contribution. Finally, have the executive director scrutinize a proof of the invitation and sign off on it.

TIME FRAME

Remember that all of the invitation planning and production has to be done well in advance. Invitations should be mailed four to six weeks before the event. Add a minimum of two weeks to have the invitations designed and about three weeks to get them printed. Allow your committee at least a week to address and mail the invitations. That means you need to start working on this at least three months before your event. If possible, add an extra month to allow for deadlines that might be missed.

GETTING THEM OUT

Set up a schedule for addressing invitations. If you have access to one, using a computer makes this job much easier. Keep a master mailing list and make a copy from which your volunteers can work.

The best way to maintain control of the mailing is to have volunteers do the mailing from a central location. As each invitation is addressed, have someone check off the name on the master list. If you can't get people to gather at a central location to address the envelopes—many people are more comfortable working at home—ask that they return the completed invitations to the office so you can mail them.

Whenever possible, committee members should add personal notes to the invitations going to personal friends. These are inserted with the invitation.

You can mail the invitations at bulk rate for two hundred invitations or more, but it requires advance planning and a permit and you will need to sort invitations into boxes according to ZIP code. You can have a mailing house do this for you, but that's an additional expense. You should determine whether the time you invest doing this will be worth what you'll save by using the bulk rate.

Once the invitations are addressed, the person in charge should personally take them to the post office. That way, you can be sure they really are mailed and not sitting on someone's kitchen table.

FOLLOW-UP CALLS

Once the invitations are out, start working the phones. Using the same master mailing list, assign portions to each committee person. All mailing lists should have phone numbers on them for just this sort of follow-up.

 TIP Following up the invitations with phone calls significantly boosts attendance.

Ideally, callers should have a script that includes a key reason for someone to attend: "I'm Jane Doherty, a volunteer with the XYZ Charity. Mrs. Smith asked me to follow up on the invitation she sent you to our event. She was sure that you would like to join her that evening. May I put you down for two seats?"

For a corporation, try something like, "I know your corporation will want to join our other corporate sponsors, which include the ABC and DEF corporations."

Typically, people wait until the last minute to decide whether or not to go to your event. Keep after them. Make a second round of calls, if necessary. Have some volunteers call business people at their offices during the day. Have others call people at home in the evening.

Promotion

The next step is to get the word out to the general public. Along with ticket sales, this is one of the most vital aspects of planning an event.

It is imperative that one very responsible person take charge of this. If you don't have a volunteer you can trust to handle it properly, consider hiring a publicist or a public relations firm, if you can afford it.

TIP PSAs (Public Service Announcements) used in combination with ticket giveaways encourage stations to get involved.

Another option: If there's a college or university in town that offers a public relations degree program, contact the department and request an intern.

Your most effective means of getting the word out is via the news media. Prepare a detailed media list. Include all radio and television stations, newspapers (weeklies, college, schools, in-house newsletters), and local magazines. Check with your local chamber of commerce and scour the "Yellow Pages" to make sure your list is comprehensive. Call each medium on the list and find out who your release should be addressed to, the specific department, the person who would handle it, and what the deadlines are. Get a fax number, too.

Prepare a concise news release and direct it to the person who handles public service announcements (PSAs) at each area radio and television station. These are 15-, 30- or 60-second spots donated by the station and usually read by an announcer. These must be short and to the point. Just give the basics (who, what, when, where, and why, and a contact).

PSAs can be written for general awareness like the ones below, or can announce an upcoming event.

SAMPLE PUBLIC SERVICE ANNOUNCEMENTS
voiced by Dick Clark for the National Parkinson Foundation

10-second radio spot:

"It can make you shake so hard you'll feel as if your heart is going to break right inside your body.

"It's Parkinson's disease.

"Let's get it before it gets you."

20-second radio spot:

"It can make you shake so hard you'll feel as if your heart is going to break right inside your body.

"It can make you so weak that you'll become a prime candidate to get heart disease. Or any of a dozen other killers.

"It's Parkinson's disease.

"Let's get it before it gets you."

30-second radio spot:

"It can make you shake so hard you'll feel as if your heart is going to break right inside your body.

"It can make you afraid to speak, even to your children. And want to hide from your friends.

"It can make you so weak that you'll become a prime candidate to get heart disease. Or any of a dozen other killers.

"It's Parkinson's disease.

"But it can be treated. Victims can be rehabilitated. And, hopefully, a cure can be found.

"Send a generous gift to The National Parkinson Foundation, P.O. Box 8822, Miami, FL.

"Let's get it before it gets you."

60-second radio spot:

"It can make you shake so hard you'll feel as if your heart is going to break right inside your body.

"It can make you tremble in sheer terror at the thought of having to speak, even to your children. And want to hide from your friends or when your own grandchildren come to visit.

"It can make you so weak that you'll become a prime candidate to get heart disease. Or any of a dozen other killers.

"It's Parkinson's disease. And that's why we ask you to help us get it before it gets you. Because as you grow older, as our population grows older, Parkinson's Disease is threatening to become a national epidemic. The number of reported cases doubled between 1970 and 1980. And yet Parkinson's can be treated. Victims can be rehabilitated. And, hopefully, a cure can be found before Parkinson's Disease strikes someone you love.

"Send a generous gift to The National Parkinson Foundation, P.O. Box 8822, Miami, FL or phone (800) 327-4545.

"Let's get it before it gets you."

FOR IMMEDIATE RELEASE CONTACT: HARRY FREEDMAN
(305) 000-0000

ESTELLE GETTY TO HOST CANCER LUNCHEON

Estelle Getty, star of "Golden Girls," "Golden Palace," and "Empty Nest" will host the annual luncheon of the Aquarius Unit of the Papanicolaou Woman's Corps for Cancer Research aboard the SS Norway on January 13, 1996. Getty, who portrayed Sophia Petrillo, garnered an Emmy for her work on the series in 1988 as well as the Golden Globe and American Comedy Awards.

The luncheon, which will take place aboard the Norway at the Port of Miami, will benefit cancer research and is sponsored by SunTrust, American Airlines, Tourneau, Norwegian Cruise Lines and Saks Fifth Avenue. 400 Miami and Fort Lauderdale business and philanthropic leaders are expected to attend the event, which will feature informal jewelry modeling and a fashion show by Saks Fifth Avenue. A special prize program of unique gifts that can be won by event-goers will be part of the luncheon. Guests at the luncheon can also qualify to win a 7-day Caribbean cruise donated by Norwegian Cruise Lines.

Tickets for the event are $75.00 and may be purchased by calling at the offices of the Woman's Corps office at 000-0000

Remember that your PSA will compete against many others for air time, so the more unusual or creative yours is, the more likely it is to be noticed. One way to do this is to have celebrities tape these messages for you. If you know a celebrity will be appearing in town, call in advance to see if he or she would be willing to tape your PSA. Arrange this through the personal manager or publicist.

Newspapers have community calendars and weekend entertainment guides. Use them. These are usually well read and can draw a great deal of attention to your event in a small space. Buy the paper for a few days and search out the departments, columns, or sections for which your event is suitable. Look for charitable causes, entertainment, features, monthly arts and events calendars, sports or education listings if they are applicable, local briefs, and any other appropriate notices you spot.

Send releases to daily newspapers four to six weeks in advance of the event. And don't assume the various departments in a newspaper swap releases. Each gets hundreds a day. Send one to each specific department. Also, send a news release to every appropriate editor. Use a cover letter. And, on the chance the paper will want to cover the event itself, send a fax reminder a day or two in advance.

For monthly magazines, the lead time for releases usually is eight weeks. For convention calendars, send information as soon as you get it, because these are often printed far in advance (quarterly or semi-annually).

For radio and television promotion, arrange for your PSA three to four weeks before the event. If possible, have a large company sponsor the cost of producing the PSA or buying air time for your message to be broadcast. In exchange, give the sponsor credit in the message.

Sometimes you can tie into public service themes run by the radio or television stations. Some stations sponsor year-long promotions, focusing on such things as children's issues, health concerns, or anti-drug campaigns. If your group fits into that

> **TIP** Ask committee members if they know people who work in the media, and try to work through them.

category, you might be able to tie in with the station's campaign. If you have corporate sponsors, ask them if they will pay for or contribute to the cost of the print advertising.

In addition to PSAs, there is news coverage. Start by distributing press kits. They should each contain copies of your:

- Cover letter
- News release
- Fact sheet
- Organization information
- Sponsor list
- Poster (if applicable)
- Photos. Use only high quality color slides (or prints) or 8x10 black-and-white glossies. Attach typed captions by taping to bottom of photograph.

FIND AN ANGLE

In most cases, no matter how important you think your event is, much of the news media won't think it's newsworthy. So how do you get coverage? Find an angle that will interest an editor. Be creative. Remember that what news media look for is what is called the "news peg," not a simple advance on the event, but some current trend or happening that might make it newsworthy. Be sure to convey what the fundraising will mean to real people.

When the South Florida Transplant Foundation planned a golf tournament in Naples, Florida, the executive director contacted an editor of the local paper's features department with an idea for a health story about a committee member whose life was saved through the organization's work. This was a good way to lead into a story about the charity and its tournament. The group got publicity first in the form of a story, then in the paper's community calendar, and again in its monthly golf publication. Had that particular angle not worked, the Transplant Foundation might have approached a medical or business editor about the cost of dialysis, how commonplace kidney transplants have become, and how they save money for insurance companies, employers, and patients.

TIME FRAME FOR PROMOTION

Four to six weeks before the event, send out the news release, mentioning the story angle briefly. Follow it up with a call to the appropriate editor, restating the story angle and offering to set up interviews with the appropriate people. Make sure you already have the name and phone number of the person to be interviewed and that the person has agreed to be interviewed and possibly photographed. You might follow up in a few days to make sure that the reporter was able to make contact with the interviewee.

Other Publicity Opportunities

Take advantage of any place that will let you post a notice of your event. A few examples: billboards, the backs of grocery store receipts, on grocery sacks and milk cartons, motel marquees, pamphlets in convenience stores, libraries, store bulletin boards, visitor centers, table displays in restaurants. Some merchants will allow you to place posters in their windows. Don't ignore area television cable companies that air community news listings or closed-circuit systems at local hotels. Be sure to check on tour guides and with movie theaters, which sometimes run announcements for charities before the film starts. In large cities, there are Web pages dedicated to charitable and other local events. Ask a computer-savvy member to research this.

Publicity Stunts

Use these judiciously. They should be offbeat, but not crazy or offensive. Using local personalities (radio disk jockeys, news anchors, etc.) can generate advance publicity. For example, for a chili cookoff, hand out free chili samples at supermarkets the week before the event.

Pre-events

Often, it is hard to succeed with the main event without doing another one first. Thus, a pre-event event can make a huge difference. A case in point: Through reading local newspapers, planners of the Miami Grand Prix knew Joan Rivers would be in Hollywood, Florida, to tape segments of the television game show, *Hollywood Squares*. The Miami

Grand Prix had committed part of the funds it raised that year to the University of Miami's Clinical AIDS Research Program. The group contacted Joan Rivers, who had previously helped raise money for AIDS programs, to see if she would be willing to attend a preview party to promote the event. She agreed. The invitations were emblazoned with "Can we talk?" (Joan Rivers's signature line), and "Meet Joan Rivers at preview event for the Miami Grand Prix." A cocktail party was held at the Grand Bay Hotel, which donated the space and food.

Prior to the party, Rivers mentioned on *Hollywood Squares* and in several local television interviews that she would be at the event. While the party normally attracted 100 to 150 people, even with race-car celebrities on hand, 500 people came. This huge attendance helped to sell in advance 75% of the tickets for the Grand Prix gala held a month later.

When the show *State Fair* went on tour prior to its 1996 Broadway opening, the promotion manager used some creative pre-events, all based on the play and its Midwestern concerns. There were pie contests in some cities, appearances by local 4-H members and their pigs and other livestock in others. In one Florida market, a TV weathercaster and his pet pot-bellied pig became one of the pre-events. The station staged a name-the-pig contest, giving tickets and show memorabilia out to participants.

Other relatively simple pre-events include having an author sign books at the local bookstore or having recording artists appear at a music store. Such pre-events draw people interested in that star to the preview, at which you should sell tickets in advance for the main event.

Talk Shows

In most communities, radio and television stations have public service shows and talk shows on which you can arrange to appear or have someone else appear on your behalf. Promote your events and your cause through careful positioning of interesting guests and celebrities on these shows. But remember that it is very important for the person who is going to represent your cause to know that he or she must talk about the event and the group itself.

The Make-A-Wish Foundation was responsible for the Miami, Florida, kickoff of artist Peter Max's "Images of an Era," a touring show of his works. Max agreed to let the first opening be a benefit for the charity, which grants wishes to children with life-threatening illnesses. Several television stations agreed to conduct live interviews during their 5 P.M. newscasts, about two hours before the Max show opened.

Earlier that day, Make-A-Wish officials prepared Max by telling him about the charity and how the money raised would be used. They provided him with a listing of basics—what the charity is, what it does, and the time and location of the show, which he spoke about on the show.

The broadcast capped a month-long media blitz. Some 3,500 people showed up that evening at the Design Center of the Americas, raising substantial funds for the charity and prompting a major contribution from the very happy owner of the gallery that presented the show.

Chapter 7 Checklist

❏ Once you have decided on an event, organize your sales force.

❏ Prepare a mailing list so you will know how many invitations to order.

❏ Equip committee members with information packets, posters, and sales pitches.

❏ Arrange for tie-in with media promotions, if possible.

❏ Buy advertising.

❏ Have invitations designed.

❏ Get bids from printers and check each one's references.

❏ Order invitations, arranging to have envelopes delivered first.

❏ Proofread invitations carefully.

❏ Have volunteers address invitations, including personal notes to people they know.

❏ Have the event coordinator/manager, or other responsible person, collect all invitations and mail them.

❏ Have sales staff follow up mailing with phone calls to those who have not yet responded.

❏ Arrange listings in community calendars (print, broadcast, and on-line), on television, at tourism bureaus, chambers of commerce, and in print media.

❏ Use World Wide Web page promotion, if available.

❏ Send e-mail reminders to those with links to the Internet.

❏ Consider buying time on an Internet provider for your celebrity (if you have one) to chat live with Internet users.

❏ Compile media list. Send press kit to each.

❏ Arrange for public service announcements at radio and television stations.

❏ Approach editors with ideas for pre-event stories.

❏ Arrange for additional publicity, such as posters, notices in utility bill mailings, on grocery receipts, in bank statements.

❏ Hold pre-event party (optional).

❏ Approach talk shows with timely ideas for a show relating to your event.

chapter **8**

FOOD FOR A CROWD

Food plays a major role in an event's success or failure, both financially and in the eyes of donors. No matter how spectacular an event looks, if the food or service is poor, that's what people are going to talk about and remember.

Food is normally the biggest expense, too, unless you have big-name entertainment, so it is critical to figure out all your options. Failure to do so can result in an event that is memorable for all the wrong reasons.

That is what happened at a $500-a-person benefit for a Southern museum. Billowing sheets of white gauze formed a Moroccan-style tent within the hotel's grand ballroom. Models in gold and silver paint served as live statues. An 18-piece band played dance music. A classical quintet stood by, poised to play during dinner, which was served at tables gleaming with china and crystal.

The organizers of this lavish spectacle took pains to see that everything—even keeping the speeches to three minutes or less—was perfect, except the most important aspect: the food. First course: A tiny squab. Next came a poached pear—tasty, but insubstantial at 9:30 P.M. after vigorous dancing and drinking. The main course: Steak au poivre with carrot soufflé. The steak was so tough that it was hard to cut with a knife, let alone chew, and it was peppery hot. The event was saved from total disgrace by a selection of rich French pastries for dessert. Uncharacteristically, the guests had plenty of room for them.

The main topic of discussion at most tables was how bad the food was. For all the planning this group had done, no one had conducted a food tasting before the event. They took it for granted that at this first-class hotel, the meal would be well prepared. As dozens of diners no doubt told the committee members, they were mistaken.

> **TIP** Steak is almost always a problem. It can be tough, it is hard to cook to everyone's liking, and still harder to deliver hot to large numbers of guests. And many cholesterol- and saturated-fat-conscious people no longer eat red meat.

There are five primary factors that determine what type of food you serve: demographics, scope, location, time, and money. Pay careful attention to each of these factors for your event and you'll narrow your food choices substantially. Let's take them one by one:

• Demographics

Who will be there and what are they likely to eat?

Even though people are now more health-conscious in their eating habits, they are still likely to make allowances when they go to expensive events. Always offer them a low-fat option, but remember that many people will nevertheless choose heartier fare. If kids are involved, don't get exotic foods. Pizza is always a hit, and hot dogs and hamburgers go over well, too.

Consider dietary restrictions and religious beliefs in planning the menu. Pork chops will offend the Hadassah group; a rich, fatty meal is not a good choice for the heart-attack recovery dinner; brandied pears are out for an Alcoholics Anonymous gathering. Also consider the charity's philosophies: Animal rights activists are likely to be outraged at being served meat.

• Scope

Are you expecting 50 people or 500? The smaller the group, the less complicated it is to plan a dinner, since you need a smaller serving staff, less equipment, and fewer dishes and rental items.

• Location

Are you planning to serve indoors or outdoors? Consider what your kitchen facilities will be and determine what is possible to prepare there.

• Time

What is appropriate to serve at the time of day you've chosen? Breakfasts are usually the lightest meal of the day, lunches a bit more substantial, dinners the most lavish. A buffet can be geared to whatever time of day you hold it.

The time of year is important to consider, too. Foods should suit the season. Out-of-season menus can be extremely costly, and in some cases, inappropriate (such as gazpacho on a wintry night).

• Money

How much can you spend? Is your main purpose making friends or raising money? If your goal is to make a profit, you should consider carefully what you spend on food. Unless it is a high-priced event or you have sufficient underwriting, choose a moderately priced but interesting meal.

How do you do that? First, think back to events at which the food was memorable. Talk to friends about their experiences, both good and bad. Then talk to the executive directors of the events at which the food was good. Inquire who and what they chose, and why. In shopping around, try out the food in all the places you consider holding your event. Hotels sometimes let you observe their other events so you can get an idea of how they might handle yours.

When you're planning the food, consider what else is going to go on during the event. For instance, if you have a ceremony or awards show planned following dinner, you'll want to get the meal over with quickly and proceed to the program. It makes sense to consult with the catering manager about how long it will take to serve the meal you are considering.

You might want to give your guests a lavish, multicourse meal, but you know it will take a long time to serve. One way to cut down on the serving time is to have your first course already set, so when guests come into the ballroom, they can start eating immediately. Also, you can start the program during that first course, getting some of the speeches done while there is no clatter of dishes to interfere.

Conversely, at an auction, bars should remain open and food should last throughout the bidding so people aren't tempted to go home once they've eaten.

Ideas for Meals, Food, and Settings

Following are some ideas to consider:

BREAKFAST
- Country style — eggs, sausage, biscuits and gravy, grits
- Pancake — pancakes, sausages or bacon, fruit
- Jewish — lox, bagels, cream cheese
- Coffee lovers — cappuccino, espresso, other specialty coffees, pastries, fruit

BRUNCH (GENERALLY BUFFET)
- Two choices each of seasonal fruits, rolls and pastries, two vegetables or salads, plus rounds of beef or turkey
- A "stations" setup, such as a pasta station, omelet station, waffle station, and a carving station where a server cuts beef, turkey, or pork to order

LIGHT LUNCH
- Salad with rolls, fruit

GOURMET LUNCH
- Chilled soup (in warm weather), elegant chicken or seafood dish, pasta or fruit salad, rich dessert

BUFFET LUNCH
- Usually ten to twelve dishes, including meats, salads, fruit, cheese, breads, and desserts

CASUAL DINNER
- Cookout with burgers and hot dogs, ribs or chicken
- Pig roast
- Fish fry
- Pasta
- Chili and cornbread
- Pizza
- Potluck or covered dish. Divide guests into three groups by last name. One group brings main courses, the next side dishes, the last desserts. Everyone should bring enough for four to six servings; the sponsoring organization usually provides the plates, silverware and beverages.

DINNER BUFFET
- Generally twenty or more choices, including

meats, salads, fruit, cheese, breads, and desserts
- Heavy hors d'oeuvres

THEME DINNERS
- Chinese, Japanese, Italian, French, Cuban, Californian, Hawaiian, Mexican, seafood, vegetarian, etc.

MISCELLANEOUS
- Afternoon tea with finger sandwiches, pastries, coffee, tea
- "Make your own" sundaes

FESTIVAL FOOD
- Chili cookoff
- Pie bakeoff
- Festival: Seafood, watermelon, chocolate, peach, tomato, apple, pumpkin, cherry, garlic, spicy foods, etc.

TASTE OF THE TOWN
- A collection of restaurants offers small samples of their appetizers, entrees, and desserts.

M E N U

CHAMPAGNE RECEPTION

Smoked Salmon and Dill Roulade
Profiteroles with Shitake duxelle
Marinated BBQ Duck
Blackened Tenderloin
Mini Crabcakes, Horseradish Mustard
Fresh Shrimp

★ ★ ★

DINNER

APPETIZER
Leek and Acorn Squash Tartlet

FISH COURSE
Pan Seared Sturgeon, Onion Marmalade Lemon Caper Sauce

INTERMEZZO
Orange Givree

ENTREE
Herb Crusted Loin Veal, Rosemary Pinot Noir Jus,
Almond Sage Rissotto, Braised Spinach and Bok Choy,
Braised Endives, Baby Carrots and Squash

DESSERT
Praline Hazelnut Vacherin

★ ★ ★

AFTER DESSERT TABLE

Dried Fruits
Petits fours
Chocolates

This is just a sample of the types of meals possible. You and your committee will know best what would be most suitable and enjoyable for the people you want to attract.

Sit-Down Meals

Banquets generally consist of three to five courses. Pick a main course and structure the rest of the meal around it. Whatever your choice, make sure you have some alternatives for those who do not eat meat or who are on special diets. Remember that people are more health-conscious than ever before, so try to achieve a balance of food groups when planning the menu.

Having an interesting meal does not have to mean spending outrageous amounts of money. Here is a sample luncheon menu that is both creative and moderately priced:

Luncheon for ±$22 per person

- Florida citrus salad with assorted field greens and raspberry vinaigrette
- Chicken Wellington, with sauce
- Julienne of fresh vegetables
- White and wild rice
- Laced doily with chocolate base filled with lemon, mango, and raspberry sorbets
- Fresh berries and coulis
- Coffee and tea

Buffets

These are the easiest types of meals to serve when you are faced with a small kitchen; a large crowd; a shortage of tables, chairs, or servers; or other circumstances in which a sit-down dinner would be difficult to pull off.

Sometimes a buffet can take longer than a sit-down meal if you don't have enough stations and it takes people a long time to get their food. Buffets also may not be appropriate if you have a formal affair. Many people do not like to carry food (especially anything with a dark sauce) across a room when they are formally dressed. In such cases, consider a modified buffet in which the first course (soup or salad) is on the table when guests are seated, the main course is served buffet style, then dessert and coffee are served at the table.

TIP Don't assume a buffet will be less expensive, especially for a small group. Buffets are often charged on a one-and-a-half portion-per-person basis rather than the single portion per person charged for a served, sit-down dinner.

Moveable Feasts

Dine-arounds, or progressive dinners, have become quite popular in recent years. Guests move from location to location for each course. Progressive dinners can be hosted in several restaurants, hotels, private homes, or a mix of the three.

The Junior League of Fort Myers, Florida, has held very successful progressive dinners for the past several years. One year, the group arranged to have three downtown locations near one another so the transitions from waterfront park, convention center, and museum were short, pleasant walks. Each venue was decorated differently and each served a course or two before the group moved on. This first-year event was so successful that it has become a much-anticipated annual happening.

Light Refreshments

Not every event calls for a whole meal. If you are on a tight budget or the event is at a time of day when no meal is called for, consider serving a variety of snacks, a wine- or alcohol-enhanced punch, and soft drinks with some munchies.

Any of the preceding options can be successful, if properly planned and executed.

Hotel Food

The greatest advantage of a hotel is that it can provide everything (food, room, setup, staging, personnel), while rented halls or other sites generally do not.

If you're working with a hotel, first set up an appointment with the catering director or banquet manager. These are people who have years of experience in planning events of varying themes for large and small groups.

Clearly communicate your needs by answering these questions: Will guests be young or old? Do they have any religious, health, or other food restrictions? Are they accustomed to eating early or late in the evening? What else is planned during the event? How long will it take to serve the courses selected?

Be prepared with the facts and figures and a reasonable estimate of how much you can spend. It is helpful to give the catering director or banquet manager a fact sheet about the organization, and some specifics about what you hope to accomplish with this event.

You might also ask that the chef attend the first meeting with you and the catering director or banquet manager to discuss menus. Usually, the catering director will suggest a choice of menus suitable for the type of people and event you plan, which affords you an estimate of food costs and allows you to negotiate to alter recipes to fit your budget. Be sure to inquire about the way the food will be presented, the size of portions, how long the meal takes to serve, and the number of service staff available.

> **TIP** Ask that the hotel not serve an identical meal for any events several weeks prior to your event.

At the initial meeting, finalize the date and which room(s) will be used for the reception and dinner. Ask to visit the hotel to observe and taste the food prior to making a commitment. Negotiate with the reservations desk on how many hotel rooms you will need for overnight guests.

Before you sign a contract, check with other organizations about their experiences with the hotels you are considering. (Remember the $500-a-plate petrified steak dinner!)

Insist on an itemized bid. Make sure everything has been covered and that there are no hidden extras. Always ask if the figure includes parking and the extra rooms needed.

Ask the banquet manager how the serving staff is usually dressed. If you want something different, expect to pay dearly for it.

Most hotels have a standard set of table linens, dishes, glassware, and silverware. If you want any thing more exotic, it will cost you extra. In most cases, so will candles, fancy candlesticks, and anything else not customarily provided. Your decorating committee or party planner can provide these, so check which would be least expensive.

> **TIP** Hotels quote meal cost separately from tax and gratuities (which can add 18% to 22%). Other items generally not included are hors d'oeuvres and beverages.

Because using a banquet room is included in the price of meals, hotels are usually particular about who gets which room. Consequently, the larger the group and the more costly the meal, the more likely it is that the hotel will give you the biggest ballroom. Don't inflate the number of people you think will come just so you can get the big room. Remember, an event that attracts 250 people will look like a failure in a room designed to hold 500.

> **TIP** If you use rental items, designate a "spotter." This person's job is to check items as they are unpacked to make sure everything is there, and to do the same thing at the end of the event, making sure everything is returned undamaged to the rental company.

Hotels usually require a guarantee a week before the event on the number of guests you expect to attend the event. The hotel uses this number to determine how much food to buy, how many people will be needed to prepare and serve, and how much setup time is needed. You normally give a final guarantee 24 to 48 hours before the event.

Once you give the guarantee, back it up in writing. This determines how many people you pay for. The hotel will charge you for at least that many guests and will add on for any extras that show up. However, if you guarantee 250 people and only 200 show, you still pay for 250.

Hotels customarily prepare for 10% more than your guarantee, so consider that when giving your figure. (They are also prepared with substitute meals for vegetarians and others with dietary restrictions.) If anything, it is better to underestimate by 10% the number you expect.

Most hotels require a 50% deposit if this is your first event with them. Organizations that have ongoing events at a particular hotel may only have to pay 10% to 20%. Deposits are usually nonrefundable. Final payment is usually due the night of the event, based on the guarantee; any additional billing follows.

Many hotels also require you to provide liability insurance or pay them a fee for coverage under their umbrella coverage.

Caterers

Outside of a hotel, you can get all these services by hiring a full-service caterer. Besides preparing the food, a full-service caterer sets up and cleans up, provides rentals and staff, and often decorations or staging.

Partial-service caterers are generally less expensive than full-service, because their services are more limited. Among the things you might have to do yourself could be renting tables and chairs, tents, and cooking equipment, hiring staff, and buying decorations. Remember to add in the costs of these things when preparing your budget.

The least expensive option is a no-service caterer who simply prepares the food and drops it off. Who serves it, how, and on what is up to you.

As with hotels, always ask the caterer to let you sample the menu you are considering. Caterers, like hotels, also ask for a guarantee for the number of people attending. They usually require a firm guarantee at least a week in advance, since they need to purchase food and coordinate the rental of any equipment, such as tables, chairs, silverware, dishes, etc. They also build a 10% cushion into the guarantee for food and rentals.

In addition to charging for food on a per-person basis, a full-service caterer charges for serving staff on an hourly basis, usually with a three-hour minimum. The number of staff is based on the number of guests attending.

Here's a basic guide for the ratio of staff to guests:
- For a sit-down meal, one server per 20 guests.
- For a buffet, one server per 40 guests.
- For sit-down or buffet, one captain per 250 guests.
- For a cocktail party, one or two bartenders per 100 guests, one or two waiters per 100 guests (depending on how extensive the menu is).

> **TIP** The exception to these numbers is when the servers are unionized, with rules that require a certain number of workers. These numbers are not negotiable no matter how worthwhile your cause.

Caterers also charge for equipment rental (and a percentage markup for acquiring it for you). Always ask what the markup will be, and ask to see the actual rental bill to ensure that you haven't been overcharged.

> **TIP** Check your contract to make sure you are not being billed twice for the same items, or charged for rental of equipment that is already on site.

Get an itemized estimate from the caterer that separates the food costs per person from all additional rentals and staff charges. There may also be a charge for cleanup crews.

Like a hotel, caterers require a deposit (which is separate from the deposit you will pay to reserve your site), and have guidelines for refunds in the event of cancellation. Make sure you know exactly what the cancellation policy is. Be sure that your caterer and event site have coordinated setup times, cleanup responsibilities, equipment usage policies, security, and parking.

As with hotels, you can be required to provide liability insurance.

> **TIP** Check with your local health department — or whatever agency inspects commercial kitchens — to see if the caterer you are considering has been cited for any health violations.

Make sure you ask the caterer what the staff will wear — usually, dark pants, white shirt, dark tie. As at hotels, if you want something different to go with your theme, you will probably have to pay for uniform rentals. Generally, it is an unnecessary expense to have special outfits, but there are times when it makes a difference.

For example, the White Party, which marked its sixteenth anniversary in 1997, is among the most recognized lavish fundraisers in the nation. It raises funds for the Health Crisis Network, an AIDS social service agency in the Miami, Florida, area. The 3,500 party tickets, which sell for $125 each, generally sell out in two days. It has also grown into a week of related events: a beach party, street party, and more, all of which raises half a million dollars for the cause.

Held on the grounds of the historic Vizcaya mansion in Miami, everything is white — the tent, the dishes, the guests' outfits, and the serving staff uniforms. If the serving staff dressed in the standard black and white, it would ruin the effect. Dressed all in white, they become virtually invisible.

While such an extra expense is probably out of

the range of most groups, this organization can afford spectacular decorations because area businesses, restaurants, and bars donate most of the food and drink. Bars and restaurants provide service staff and all liquor is donated.

In deciding on your menu, let the experts help. A banquet manager or caterer designs several meals a day for many types of occasions. Their experience can help you, and it could stimulate ideas to make your event unusual. Keep in mind that theirs are only suggestions, and that you can modify them according to your tastes and budget. In doing so, however, remember that these people regularly deal with large groups and know how to meet their needs.

Doing It Yourself

Hotels and caterers are not the only ones who can prepare a meal. Another option is either doing it yourself or using a group of volunteers. That means you figure out how much food to buy, shop for it, find a place to prepare it, prepare it, serve it, and clean it up. You will still need to rent dishes, tablecloths, silverware, and often the serving ovens and other related equipment.

When you begin designing your menu, remember there has to be a balance to the food. For example, if you have a Mexican night, consider that not everyone eats spicy foods, so you should have some mild dishes as well. At a Japanese dinner, not everyone will eat sushi, so also offer tempura or a plainly cooked fish with choice of sauces for those who like their food cooked.

Besides appealing to a broad range of tastes, there are visual and textural facets to consider. Try to design each course so that there is a variety of color and texture.

Before finalizing your menu and shopping for supplies, consider your limitations. How extensive a kitchen will you have? How much help and equipment will you have? How skilled is your cooking staff? It is not a good idea to attempt something that is labor- and space- intensive, such as paella, if you will be working in a home kitchen.

When you're doing your own cooking, try to choose recipes that are as simple as possible and that use as little equipment as possible. If a recipe calls for stirring until something boils, someone will wind up stirring for ages waiting for a big pot to boil. And don't plan to have fresh vegetables like string beans or mushrooms, which require individual cutting or cleaning. If the first and second courses need to be served hot, make sure you have enough burners and room to heat them both on the stove at once.

Will you be able to fit everything into the oven that needs to be in there at once? And don't forget about refrigerator and freezer space. Will there be enough room so that all your perishable goods will fit in?

Once you have an idea of what you would like to make, stage a tasting, just like hotels and caterers do. Involve everyone who will be cooking. Try out all the recipes. This small-scale version of your meal will help you work out problems you might otherwise not foresee.

Don't get too exotic — tasty simple fare beats ill-prepared exotic dishes every time.

> **TIP** Pay attention to the seasonality of some foods. Peaches may be cheap when you try out your menu in July, but will be astronomically expensive in October — if you can get them at all.

Once you finalize the menu, go through each recipe and list all the ingredients you will need to buy. Don't forget cleaning supplies, paper towels, sponges, dishwashing liquid, garbage bags, etc. Figure out what is already available and how to arrange getting everything to the event site.

Next, prepare your shopping list. Do your multiplication at home, not in the supermarket aisles. For example, for a sit-down dinner, figure on six to eight ounces of chicken, fish, or meat per person, perhaps a bit less for banquets.

However, portion size can depend on your event. If you're putting on a dinner after an athletic competition or other strenuous activity such as a dance contest, plan on heartier appetites. If the event is lengthy and dinner will not be served until the end, consider serving a light snack early in the schedule.

Take your recipes with you when you shop. Shop systematically, using a calculator to double-check your figures. When possible, go to a food co-op or wholesale discount store to purchase food. Look for sales. Ask the manager whether you can get a discount for large-quantity purchases. (And if you have to pick up more food than you can handle alone, arrange to have two or more people meet you at the supermarket.) If there is a store in your area that's open 24 hours a day, go when it is quiet so you and your six shopping carts do not become a logistical nightmare. Don't buy perishables more than a few days before the event.

> **TIP** Liability is a very important consideration when you prepare the food on your own, should it spoil. The more cooks and varieties of storage, the more likely it is to occur.

TIME SAVERS

There are lots of time-savers at your disposal. Use as many as you can. Prepare soups and beverages in advance, using about a quarter of the liquid needed. Transfer to a pot (or pitcher, for drinks), then add the rest of the liquid. Transport them to the event site already cooled.

Frozen pie crusts save time in both preparation and cleanup (no pie plates to wash). Presliced meats and breads and frozen vegetables all help cut preparation time.

> **TIP** When possible, arrange for some food to be prepared in advance at the homes of your cooks. (But do this only with cooks whose kitchens are adequate to handle this kind of preparation, and who maintain basic health standards.)

AT THE SITE

On the day of the event, bring in everything you will need. If possible, have foods sliced and cleaned at people's homes before being brought to the event site. Post the menu, cooking schedule, and assignment of tasks in a central location where everyone can refer to them. Use the best cooks for the big jobs; let the less culinarily inclined wash dishes and cut fruits or vegetables.

> **TIP** Place garbage cans or bags in various places in the kitchen so no one will have to go far to find one. This lets you clean up as you go.

IF DISASTER STRIKES

Sometimes, no matter how well you planned, something goes wrong. Always have someone taste dishes before they are served. That way, only a few people will taste the failures. But there will come a time when someone uses salt instead of sugar, cornstarch instead of flour, burns something beyond recognition, or simply drops it on the floor.
Rule One: Stay calm.

Rule Two: No matter how desperate you are, don't serve it. Instead, send someone out for some extras to fill in. A few possibilities:

- Assorted cheese and crackers
- Pre-cooked meats (ham, salami, chicken, turkey) rolled into tubes (stuffed with cream cheese is optional)
- Assorted fruits (apples, orange wedges, grape clusters)
- Quick-cooking rice or pasta
- Frozen vegetables (canned is not a suitable substitute)
- Breads or crackers, butter and jam, or cheese spread
- Trays of store-bought cookies and chocolates
- Assorted frozen yogurts and gourmet ice cream

Liquor and Other Beverages

The first question to ask is whether you should serve alcohol at all. Unless you have a cash bar, alcohol will be a large expense. If you hold the event somewhere other than a hotel and have to buy the liquor yourself, that means a considerable outlay of money. And there is also the potential liability if someone gets drunk at your event, then has a car accident on the way home. More states are passing laws that allow victims and their families to sue not only the person who was intoxicated, but whoever served the liquor, the group that hired the bartender, and the group's board of directors.

When you do serve liquor, always try to make sure people don't drink too much and that cabs are available for those who should not drive home. Have volunteers or paid staff serve as spotters, looking for those who have overindulged and need a ride home. Usually, the organizations pays for the expense of the taxi fare. Also, forget the notion that coffee sobers you up; it doesn't.

The selection of beverages is determined by the type of event you have, the ages of those attending, and your menu. At most fancy banquets, dances, and other such events for adults, it is customary for alcohol to be available, either at a cash bar or as wine served at the table. Still, at most events there is now an ample assortment of nonalcoholic beers and light alcohol punches as well as wine coolers, spritzers, sodas, and fruit juices.

Hotels usually charge per drink or per bottle for alcoholic and nonalcoholic beverages. Most hotels will not let you bring in donated wine or champagne, or if they do, they are likely to charge you a corkage fee of $2 or a percentage of the value of each bottle.

Cash bars are becoming more common, both as a form of limiting intake, since they require people to seek out and pay for their drinks, and as a way to cut liquor costs (see below). Cash bars also reduce the number of servers you need. You can also keep the cocktail hour short — they used to run about 90 minutes, but most groups limit them to an hour. Skip the after-dinner drinks and the decanters of wine on the table. Or close the bar once dinner starts (and count on hearing a lot of complaints.)

At some events, certain drinks go with the food served and can be big moneymakers. A few examples: Beer at a chili festival, Chianti with a spaghetti dinner, margaritas with a Mexican meal. Serve the drinks, but do so in moderation. For example, at many sporting events, liquor service is halted at half-time.

As pointed out above, liquor is expensive, and this is another good reason to ask if you really want to serve it. At a 200-person event, for example, you will need two bottles of wine per table of ten. At $20 a bottle times 20 tables, wine alone could cost $400. If people want other alcoholic beverages, the hotel or caterer will probably charge $2.75 or more per drink. The average person drinks two drinks. At $2.75, that's another $1,000. Then you have to add two bars, bartenders, and setups. That's another $300. Already, your expenses are $1,700 just for liquor (not including tax and gratuity) — more than $8.50 per person. A cash bar can substantially offset this cost. By charging $3 per drink, you cover the bulk of the cost of cocktails and wine.

Soft drinks are necessary even if you do serve

```
    EO# 000030292            EVENT ORDER          DATE: THU. MAR  9,1995
    ------------------------------------------------------------------------
    FUNCTION: PAPANICOLAOU CANCER RESEARCH    TYPE : RECEPTION
    POST AS :                                 MGR  KATHRYN C. MURRAY
    CONTACT : MR. HARRY FREEDMAN              PHONE: 305-454-8375
              3800 South Ocean Drive
              Suite 242
              Hollywood, Fl 33019
    BILLING : SOCIAL                                    ACCOUNT: 3032095
    ------------------------------------------------------------------------
       TIME            ROOM                            GUARANTEE    SET
    11:00 A - 11:45    FLORENTINE D/R                     350       400
    ------------------------------------------------------------------------
    FOOD:
    Hors D'Oeuvres to be passed - Type to be advised

    BEVERAGE:
    TO BE PASSED AS GUESTS ENTER

    Mimosas                                          6.00    Each
    White Wine                                      24.00    P/BOTTLE
    Bloody Marys                                     4.75    EACH
    Assorted Fruit Juices - (Orange, Cranberry, Apple) 2.25  EACH
    Perrier with Lime                                2.75    EACH

    SET UP:
    2 Registration Tables outside Room with Lamps
    15 Cocktail Tables with Chairs
    1 Raffle Table
    Raffle Drum Needed

    LINEN:
    Linen Color to be advised                        1.50    P/Person

    MISCELLANEOUS:
    Photographer - Lucien Capart

    SPECIAL NOTES:
    Vallet Parking
    ------------------------------------------------------------------------



    All food & beverage prices are subject to 19% service charge & 6% tax.

    A guarantee figure must be given 48 hours prior to the function.  If
    the count is not received at that time, THE BREAKERS will use the
    estimated figure as the final guarantee.

    Arrangements Accepted By: _____
```

alcohol. A good selection includes both regular and sugar-free cola, lemon-lime sodas, ginger ale, and colas that are also caffeine-free (in regular and sugar-free versions); plus iced tea, bottled water, and fruit juices. Other possibilities include fruit-juice spritzers, lemonade, fresh cider, milkshakes, and ice-cream sodas. Coffee and tea (regular and decaf for both) should be available, too. At outdoor events, especially when the weather is warm, make sure there is plenty of cold water available.

> **TIP** Sometimes hotels will allow you to bring in donated wine and bottled waters if you have a cash bar. Caterers are more likely to let you bring in your own wine and liquor, since it's one less thing for them to worry about.

How much coffee, soda, and alcohol do you need? The general rules of thumb for beverages are:

- Coffee: One pound makes about 60 cups
- Champagne: One case pours 45 to 50 glasses
- Liquor: One quart makes 25 to 30 drinks
- Punch: One gallon makes 24 cups

In terms of consumption, people generally drink less wine than beer, and less beer than soft drinks. For alcoholic drinks, figure about two drinks per person each hour.

A few ways to cut your beverage expenses include:

- Beer costs less in a keg than in bottles or cans. When possible (and practical), consider kegs. (Remember that they can be messy and slow, so they may not work well at all events.)
- In getting quotes on hard liquor, ask if the price is based on house brands (the cheapest), name or call brands (more expensive brands), or premium brands. Specify what brands to use and how much liquor should be poured per drink.
- Instead of either a free bar or a cash bar, provide two drink tickets per paid guest. After that, guests pay for their own drinks.
- Specify that you be charged based on the number of open bottles of liquor served.

When you serve alcohol, keep in mind that there are legal issues to consider. In some states, you have to have a permit to hold an open bar. Serving liquor to minors is illegal. Doing so can cause you legal trouble as well as draw disfavor from the pub-

lic. And there are the previously mentioned issues of liability in connection with accidents that happen when guests leave your event. Make sure you know what the laws are in your area, and make sure you rigidly adhere to them.

Feeding Staff and Volunteers

Have your staff and volunteers eat before they arrive at the event. It saves time, money, and effort. But if they are going be there a long time (setting up or cleaning up), you will need to feed them. At a hotel, you can ask if the chef could provide a simple dish — such as pasta and salad — in a room away from the event itself. Make sure you have beverages (coffee, soda, juice) available throughout the working period for anyone who is helping to set up. It is cheaper if you can provide these yourself (bring them in ice chests), but some hotels won't allow it.

Leftovers

Invariably, there is leftover food. With so many homeless and hungry people, you can often make arrangements to donate leftovers to a soup kitchen or shelter. Hotels and caterers generally won't do this for you, so you need to make your own arrangements. Plan on supplying containers and delivery. (You can get a receipt from the charity for the donation.) It is a nice touch to mention this in the program or announce it at the event.

Tipping

The general rule on tipping is that 18% is added on to your bill and divided accordingly: Fourteen percent to the waiters and bartenders, 3% to captains and maitre d's, 1% to the catering director. For exemplary service you can tip as much as 22%.

If people really go out of their way to help with unexpected problems, you might want to give them something extra. If the service is excellent and you think you might want to hold another event there, give the maitre d'hôtel or headwaiter something extra (about $100). Tip any particularly good wait-

> **TIP** Check to see if you have been charged tax. As a nonprofit organization, you are exempt.

ers as well (about $50). Caution: Don't give these extras to the catering director to distribute, because he or she may not get it to the right people.

Food as the Main Event

While food is often part of a larger event, it can also be the reason for an event. (See also Chapter 1, Finding an Event That Fits.) Let's face it, people love to eat and giving them what they love can mean big money.

One popular type of food event is the chili festival. These are held all over the country, and attract from 100 to 300 entrants, each with their beloved chili recipes, and each of whom pays $50 or so to enter. Each entrant gets a booth in which to cook. Events of this kind can raise upwards of $200,000 for the charity. Often, a chili festival can be tied in with a country-and-western concert.

There are all types of food events you can stage. Pick a theme: Italian, Mexican, chocolate, seafood, garlic, even area restaurant specialties. You reserve the site, rent booths to vendors, and charge people admission to enter. Add some music, crafts booths, and a nice setting, and you are likely to make a lot of money while giving people a good time.

Chapter 8 Checklist

❏ Assess the event's market, scope, location, time, and budget. Determine what sort of food is appropriate.

❏ Develop list of hotels or caterers. Visit each and meet with the catering director to discuss possible menus and costs. (If you are doing your own cooking, have your committee meet to discuss menus and try out recipes.)

❏ Negotiate the contract.

❏ If you are using a caterer, determine what equipment your staff or volunteers will need to rent. Assign a person to oversee this.

❏ A week before the event, provide an attendance guarantee for the hotel or caterer. Finalize this in writing two days before the event.

❏ If you are preparing your own food, develop the shopping list and arrange for people to shop and cook.

❏ Determine what beverages will be served.

❏ Arrange for meals or snacks for the staff who will set up the site.

❏ Prepare and serve food.

❏ Arrange to take leftovers to a homeless shelter or food kitchen.

❏ Tip serving staff an additional amount if service was good and you plan to use the hotel or caterer again.

Bringing stars to town for your special event can be a dazzling way to attract attention and money, drawing in people who may have been unaware of your cause. But it can also cause a disaster of stellar proportions. Before deciding on a celebrity event, take into consideration the myriad hidden costs and requirements attached. It may be worth the extra effort, but remember that star power can create magic—or a black hole where your budget used to be.

chapter 9

POWER OF THE STARS

The Cost of a Free Appearance

In many cases, celebrities are generous with their time and will offer to appear without charge. For a big-name star, that might mean a savings of $70,000. Or does it? It's easier—and far less expensive—to have a comedian walk out on stage, have a chef demonstrate a cooking technique, or a sports figure sign autographs, than it is to bring in a singer or dancer. If the star appears with a 20-piece band, it is likely to cost your group plenty (the going rate is about $50 an hour per musician, $75 an hour for overtime, plus transportation, hotels, food, etc.). Even though the celebrity is donating his or her time, you will still have to pay the band members to rehearse for three to five hours, as well as to perform.

Then add in the costs of staging, lighting, sets, and props. That "free" entertainment can wind up costing $20,000 or more. Again, look at the celebrity's contract. In it you will find a rider which is a list of requirements for producing the show.

If you have never planned a complicated celebrity concert before (producing a school play does not count), spend the $500 or so to have an attorney look over the contract. Consider that stars normally have 20- to 30-page contracts, with riders listing their individual requirements for appearance. Each star's contract also includes such things as the way they must travel (usually first class); their accommodations (usually a suite); how many people travel in their entourage (anywhere from one to 30, including makeup artists, hairdressers, personal valets, musicians, tour managers, and assorted "others"); the entourage's travel and lodging requirements; what meals must be provided and what foods should be served; cancellation clauses; and anything else the star requires. Furthermore, laws vary from state to state, so be sure you hire an attorney who is familiar with entertainment and contract laws. It could save you thousands of dollars later.

Another option: Ask the business manager of a regional theater to review it for you.

Lining Up a Celebrity

After you have carefully analyzed your group's budget and know how much you can spend (see Chapter 2, The Matter of Money), you must then decide if it's worth the time, energy, and trouble it will take to get a star, and whether the celebrity is really going to attract many more people. Usually, the answer is yes, especially for first-time events or those that are competing with many others for attention.

The next step is to figure out what star will best suit your event. There are all sorts of celebrities—local sports stars and media personalities, politicians, chefs, artists, authors, directors, singers, dancers. It is easier to get a local figure to appear at an event in his or her hometown, and also considerably cheaper, since there will be no airfare or hotel bills. But if you want something bigger, say a national or international star, think about the nature of the event and whether the person you are considering makes sense for that event.

When you think over your choices, it is imperative that you keep your budget firmly in mind. If you have only $3,000 for entertainment, strike off the list mega stars like Diana Ross, the cast of "Stomp," and David Copperfield. If you are considering a sports celebrity auction, you could manage on a modest budget if you invite a local sports or media personality to be the auctioneer, then ask various sporting goods stores or teams for donations of jerseys, hats, balls, tickets, and so on. More and more local celebrities, including sports figures, command fees of as much as $7,000 for appearances, autograph signings, and endorsements.

Musical acts, such as Tony Bennett or Liza Minelli can cost from $55,000 to $150,000 (add $5,000 for the travel expenses of staff and key musicians). Comedians like Robin Williams, Billy Crystal, Jay Leno, or Phyllis Diller can cost within the same range, but with lower staff travel expense. For stars like Rosie O'Donnell, Fran Drescher, Jerry Seinfeld, Mariah Carey, or Patti LaBelle, the figures climb to astronomical levels.

If you hope to bring in more than one celebrity and your entertainment budget is tight, consider trying to negotiate a "favored nations" clause. (A job for your lawyer.) This clause ensures that if two or more stars appear, all are treated equally. They are paid the same amount, and they get the same accommodations, amenities, and billing. Sometimes you (or your attorney) can also negotiate a lower fee because the celebrities want to work together, or because yours is a prestigious event, or a cause they support.

The American Cancer Society used this clause successfully at a benefit opening of the Hilton Hotel in Miami at which Rita Moreno and David Brenner appeared. Each usually charged about $22,500 per appearance for charity events in the 1970s. (These days, the numbers would be higher. Check with their agents or management firms.) The charity had a $30,000 budget provided by Hilton. By doing some research, the charity knew both celebrities would already be in town, so it offered them "favored nations" contracts that would pay each

> **TIP** You can save money if someone else has already hired the star and provided transportation. If the star must stay longer for your event, you'll then only be responsible for the additional hotel expense and possibly airfare home.

$15,000, plus rooms and airfare for themselves and their entourages. Brenner and Moreno wanted to work together, and so they agreed to the clause.

Reading the Stars

Lining up celebrities requires creativity and research. You are most likely to convince them to appear at your event if it is a charity in which they have a personal interest, or if they are going to be in your area at the time of the event, and if you can afford their fee (possibly through corporate underwriting).

There are many ways to get this information. The most accessible source is television. Watch the talk shows, entertainment news shows, and televised benefits. Stars often discuss their interests and upcoming schedules on these shows.

Read the supermarket tabloids. There may be a lot of "Space aliens abducting male first-borns"-type stories, but the tabloids also carry information about the charity work celebrities do. Both the tabloids and conventional newspapers have written many stories about Dionne Warwick, Elton John, Stevie Wonder, Gladys Knight, Elizabeth Taylor, and Sharon Stone, all of whom have taken active roles in AIDS-related fundraising because of the disease's devastating impact on the entertainment industry. Dick Clark works tirelessly for the National Parkinson Foundation because a relative has Parkinson's disease. Rikki Lake is an outspoken advocate for animal welfare causes. Ted Danson is active in defending the environment. And, of course, Jerry Lewis is synonymous with the Muscular Dystrophy Association, whose telethon he hosts every year.

Celebrity Service publishes a newsletter that lists which stars are doing what projects, movies, and appearances. The service is expensive (several thousand dollars per year), but if you plan a lot of events with a lot of celebrities, it pays to subscribe. (See Chapter 12, Tools of the Trade.)

Contact local theaters and performing arts centers, as well as civic centers and convention halls, within a 500-mile radius of your town. Ask for a list of what stars might be appearing at their facilities, and make a seasonal or year-long schedule of celebrities who will be at local venues. Most of these locations publish lists of their upcoming seasons, so you will need to collate the information they provide. Remember that it costs a lot less to bring in someone from a nearby city than it does from a distant coast.

Ask the star's publicist for a schedule of performances, then schedule your event around those dates.

For example, in New York City, many charity events take place on Monday nights because the theater people are off then and thus are available for special appearances.

Similarly, make note of what dates to avoid. Don't schedule a sports event—or anything else, if you can help it—on a weekend when there's a big game. You'll waste all your star power.

Harnessing Star Power

Once you have determined which celebrities may be interested in your charity and may also be nearby, it's time to invite them to appear. You could take the usual route and call a booking agent. Don't. He is a middle man who generally makes 10% or more of the amount he books the celebrity for, and so is looking to get the highest appearance fee possible. The booking agent also negotiates with the agency that represents the artist. The agency also gets a percentage, and so the agent there will also want to get the highest amount possible.

Then the agent from the representing agency goes to the star's personal manager, who also gets a percentage. . . .

At this point, there are three people between you and the celebrity, each one of whom is interested in making as much money as possible. Go this route and you're sure to pay top dollar.

Some of the larger watchmakers, such as Tourneau and Piaget, and jewelers might agree to donate a watch or piece of jewelry for an upscale charity event. Offer that as an in-kind honorarium for the celebrity's appearance.

There are also ways to reduce the number of middlemen. First, if someone in your organization knows the star, contact that person and ask him or her to explain to the star the charitable cause you represent. This often works if you happen to know that the charity is one in which the celebrity is interested.

The best route is generally through a celebrity's publicist. Most celebrities have a publicist, whose job it is to get the star media exposure. The publicist gets a regular retainer, rather than a percentage of

THE BUSINESS OF SPECIAL EVENTS

Celebrity Inquiry Letter

January 2, 1996

Mr. William Samuels
The Bill Samuels Organization
P.O. Box 000
Beverly Hills, CA 90213

Attn: Annie

RE: CHANTAL

Dear Bill,

I am well aware that Chantal must receive thousands of requests every year to lend her name to charities, or to perform at their fund-raisers. However, the true-life nature of this young girl's story, along with Chantal's involvement in the film "Mask" made us think of her immediately for a very special event that we are currently planning.

Catherine Connelly was born with severe facial birth defects (see attached photo documentation), which resulted in her having essentially few or no recognizable features. There are tens of thousands of other children who are born with similar birth defects, as well as children and adults who often need extensive facial reconstructive surgery due to forms of cancer.

I have enclosed pictures and background material which speak more eloquently to the hardships these children face than words ever could.

We have an excellent chance to help Catherine Connelly and thousands like her, by the creation of a very special and highly visible event, which will take place at Palm Beach's Mar-a-Lago Club on Sunday, April 14th, 1996. Since this event is being held at one of the most visible private clubs in the world, during its opening season, we expect to attract a large number of affluent social and business leaders.

The involvement of Chantal at Mar-a-Lago would assure a sell-out and highly financially successful fund-raiser during this critical year. We would hope Chantal would agree to be our honored guest, along with Alexandra Kennedy, who has already agreed to be involved. Of course, we would provide 1st class travel and accommodations, and Mr. Trump will certainly provide suites at Palm Beach's historic Mar-a-Lago Club.

We are also expecting wide-spread national media attention to the issue of children with severe medical problems and the current insurance situation in this country. Many of these children can receive donated reconstructive surgery, but all hospitals require a minimum of $50,000 or more in advance for surgical suites and other hospital related costs.

There is interest by both *People Magazine* and *The Oprah Winfrey Show* to talk about these "children without faces" and the Connelly Foundation's groundbreaking work. Chantal could be our "celebrity hero." Her participation and acceptance of this invitation prior to January 1st could have a tremendous impact on our ticket sales and public relations efforts.

Catherine is still awaiting several surgical procedures, and there are countless other children just beginning this long process. They are depending on the support of projects such as this and the generosity of individuals and corporations to enable them to walk among their peers with a true smile on their face, rather than to be subject to countless stares and comments.

I would be happy to meet with you to answer any questions or concerns about this project. Please be assured that, since the event is at Mar-a-Lago, everything about the evening will be first class. Also, our goal is to have 100% of our costs covered by corporate or individual underwriting or through donated services.

Now that Chantal is living at least part of the year in Florida, we are hopeful that she would be willing to give a single Sunday evening to change the lives of thousands of "children without faces." If she is not able to attend, perhaps she would be willing to lend her support and her name to this cause as part of the honorary committee, and/or make a public service announcement for the Foundation.

I look forward to hearing from you regarding Chantal's participation in this very important fundraising event.

Sincerely,

Harry A. Freedman

Enclosure

Sample Contract Request Letter for a Celebrity

February 4, 1997

Mr. Mark Smith
The Mark Smith Co.
100 N. Roberts Blvd., Suite A
Berverly Hills, CA 90211

Dear Mark:

This letter authorizes you to proceed towards contract for SHANNON MILLER IN
CONCERT. Ms. Miller would perform with her musicians on Friday, April 18, 1997
at approximately 10:00 p.m., in the Main Ballroom of the Omni International Hotel,
Miami, Florida.

This Gala evening is a benefit for the University of Miami/Jackson Memorial Burn
Center. The Mailman Center for Child Development and The Learning Experience
School, and is the kick-off event for the Miami Grand Prix. The Grand Prix Gala,
which is attended by approximately 1,000 people, has become recognized as one of
the premiere international events of the Miami social season.

We would like to make an offer not to exceed Twenty-five Thousand Dollars
($25,000), which would include the services by Ms. Miller and her musicians as a
self-contained act. We would expect Ms. Miller to perform for a minimum of one
hour; there will be no opening act. The Twenty-Five Thousand Dollars ($25,000)
offer is for Ms. Miller and her musicians only. We would be responsible for
providing appropriate air transportation for her musicians and support personnel,
not to exceed 16 people (2 first-class, 14 coach). We would also provide first-class
accommodations at the Omni International Hotel (1 suite, 15 singles), as well as
sound and lights as appropriate within the Ballroom setting of the Hotel.

We would certainly also like to explore the possibility of having the opportunity of
promoting Ms. Miller's new album in conjunction with the Grand Prix Gala and
Grand Prix Weekend. We certainly would be delighted to have her participate as
Grand Prix Marshall prior to the Grand Prix race on Sunday, April 20.

I look forward to an early response so we may begin to publicize Ms. Miller's
participation in the appropriate manner.

Sincerely,

Harry A. Freedman
Coordinator - Grand Prix Gala

Papanicolaou Woman's Corps
for Cancer Research, Inc.

FAX MEMORANDUM

TO: Dee Dee Berkowitz
           DMB Speaker's Bureau

FROM: Harry Freedman
           Papanicolaou Woman's Corps

DATE: October 31, 1994

RE: **SALLY JESSY RAPHAEL CONTRACT**

Enclosed is a faxed copy of the contract and check for Sally Jessy Raphael's speaking engagement for our "Women Who Lead" awards luncheon on Thursday, March 9, 1995.

I also have enclosed copies of correspondence for this event and draft samples of our "SAVE THE DATE" card.

As we discussed, I need photos of Sally Jesse Raphael in order to complete our "SAVE THE DATE" cards and to go with our press releases. As you know, the "season" gets jam packed in Palm Beach so the eaarlier we get information out to committee and press, the better the response.

Thanks!!!

Regional Office • The Hallmark Building • 3800 South Ocean Drive • Suite 242 • Hollywood FL 33019 • (305) 454-8375 • Fax (305) 454-9858

The Papanicolaou Woman's Corps has been supporting cancer research since 1952

October 20, 1994

Mr. Harry Freedman
Papanicolaou Woman's Corps for Cancer Research
3800 South Ocean Drive, suite 242
Hollywood, FL 33019

Dear Harry:

It is with great pleasure that I enclose the agreement for **Sally Jessy Raphael** to speak at the *WOMEN WHO LEAD* luncheon on **Thursday March 9, 1995.** Please sign **BOTH** copies and return **BOTH** copies to me. I will countersign and return a fully executed copy to you for your files.

Also enclosed is a Questionnaire. Please complete and return it at your earliest convenience. Sally will use this information to customize her presentation.

Publicity photographs and a biography will follow under separate cover.

I am delighted to provide this exciting, notable speaker for your Palm Beach audience and feel confident that her appearance will be a great success.

Thank you once again for the opportunity to work with you and the Papanicolaou Woman's Corps for Cancer Research on this event. If you have any questions, please do not hesitate to call. If I am not available, my assistants Helen Hill or Marisol Mendoza will be able to help.

Sincerely,

DeeDee Berkowitz
DDB/hh

Encl.

7800 RED ROAD, SUITE

INVOICE

October 20, 1994

Mr.Harry Freedman
Papanicolaou Woman's Corps for Cancer Research
3800 South Ocean Drive,suite 242
Hollywood, FL 33019

Invoice #   **FL-PWCC-01**

The following represents a deposit of fee due for the speaking engagement of **Sally Jessy Raphael** on **Thursday March 9, 1995.**

TOTAL SPEAKING FEE		**$27,500.00**
DEPOSIT DUE BY	**November 11, 1994**	$13,750.00
BALANCE DUE	On or Before TWO Business Days Prior to Engagement	$13,750.00

Please send and make check payable to DMB Speakers Bureau Inc.
Federal I.D. number   65-00223201
Late charges will be assessed on all invoices received past the due date.

Any other pertinent expenses will follow

THANK YOU

7800 RED ROAD, SUITE 211 MIAMI, FLORIDA 33143

SPONSOR AGREEMENT

This agreement entered into as of this __20th__ day of __October__ 1994 by and between **DMB SPEAKERS BUREAU INC.**, 7800 Red Road - suite 211, Miami, Florida 33143 (hereinafter referred to as "DMB") and **Papanicolaou Woman's Corps for Cancer Research, Inc.** (hereinafter referred to as "Sponsor").

DMB agrees to provide the services of the Contractor at the time and place and subject to the terms and conditions set forth below:

TERMS OF ENGAGEMENT for Job# FL-PWCC-01

Contractor: Sally Jessy Raphael   Date: Thursday March 9, 1995

Time: 11:00 a.m. Sponsors Reception   **Topic:** TBD
                  12.00 noon Luncheon
                  1.30 p.m.   Presentation

Length of Engagement: 45 minutes

Engagement Location: The Breakers   (407) 655-6611
                            1, South County Road
                            Palm Beach, FL 33480

Sponsor Contact: Mr. Harry Freedman   (305) 454-8375
                            Papanicolaou Woman's Corps for Cancer Research
                            3800 South Ocean Drive, suite 242
                            Hollywood, FL 33019

Other Specific Requirements:
· Sponsor will provide first-class, round trip air transportation for two N.Y.- West Palm Beach - N.Y.
· Sponsor will provide hotel accommodations for two (1 suite +1 single) on the night before engagement
· Sponsor will provide all ground transportation by private limousine
· Sponsor will provide audio/visual equipment to fit needs of Contractor's presentation
· Contractor will customize presentation for Papanicolaou Woman's Corps for Cancer Research

FEE: **$27,500.00**
DEPOSIT: **$13,750.00** 50% PAYABLE WITH SIGNED AGREEMENT by November 11, 1994
BALANCE: **$13,750.00**   PAYABLE ON OR BEFORE Two business days prior to engagement
        Please send and make all checks payable to DMB Speakers Bureau Inc.
        Federal Identification number 65-0223201

Expenses are the sole responsibility of Sponsor, will be billed separately and are subject to the terms stated (including late charges) on the invoice. Expenses will include transportation charges (air fare, if necessary), lodging and meals, taxicab or limousine fares and any other expenses specified in this Agreement or made necessary by the Contractor's trip to and from the city in which the program is presented.

In addition to the above, both DMB and Sponsor agree that:
No Publication. Sponsor agrees not to publicize this program until Sponsor has paid the deposit and received a signed copy of the Agreement from DMB.

Agency Relationship. DMB is acting as an independent agent in arranging this program and

MIAMI CHICAGO

QUESTIONNAIRE

It is important that your speaker receive as much information as possible prior to your meeting to aid in their speech preparation.

Please complete this form and return as soon as possible.

1. SPEAKER: _Sally Jessy Raphael_

2. DATE OF MEETING: _March 9, 1995_

3. NAME OF YOUR ORGANIZATION: _Papanicolaou Woman's Corps for Cancer Research, Inc._

4. EVENT: _"Women Who Lead" Awards Luncheon_

5. MAJOR OBJECTIVE OF THIS MEETING: _Fundraising for Cancer Research_

6. ATTIRE: _Upscale Business Attire_

7. NAME AND TITLE OF THE INTRODUCER: _Ann Bishop, News Anchor, Channel 10/ABC_

8. WHAT IS THE EXACT SCHEDULE OF EVENTS FOR THIS SPEAKER?

    11 A.M. VIP Reception/Photos
    12 P.M. Luncheon
    1:15 P.M. Speaker and Award Presentation

9. AUDIENCE DEMOGRAPHICS:

    A. SIZE OF AUDIENCE: _500_ B. MEN: _30%_ C. WOMEN: _70%_

    D. AGES: _25 - 75_ E. GENERAL DESCRIPTION OF ATTENDEES:
    Busines and Social Leaders, Local and Regional Philanthropists

10. WHO SPOKE AT THIS MEETING LAST YEAR? _First time event_

11. IF THIS SPEAKER COULD LEAVE YOUR GROUP WITH TWO THOUGHTS WHAT WOULD THEY BE?
    What are the characteristics of a woman leader.

7800 RED ROAD, SUITE 211, MIAMI, FLORIDA 33143

12. SPEAKER'S CONTACT PRIOR TO MEETING:

    NAME: _Harry Freedman_ TITLE: _Executive Director Papanicolaou Woman's Corps_

    TELEPHONE:(WORK) _305-454-8375_ (HOME) _305-754-4405_

13. SPEAKER'S CONTACT AT MEETING:

    NAME: _same as above_ TITLE: _____

    TELEPHONE:(WORK) _____ (HOME) _____

If there are any changes in the agenda or subject matter, please advise us as soon as possible. Thank you for you time and cooperation.

Please mail of fax this form to:

DMB SPEAKERS BUREAU INC.
7800 Red Road
Suite# 211
Miami, Florida 33142
FAX (305) 662-9965

SAMPLE CELEBRITY CONTRACT

Agreement made as of _____ between _____ (hereinafter referred to as "Company") for the services of _____ (hereinafter referred to as "Artist") and _____ _____ (hereinafter referred to as "Purchaser").

It is mutually agreed between the parties as follows:

Purchaser hereby engages Company and Company hereby accepts such engagement to furnish Artist to perform, upon all of the terms and conditions herein set forth.

1.   ENGAGEMENT:
(a)   Artist shall perform a lecture at a dinner function in the ballroom at the _____ on _____ at approximately 8:30 PM, at the _____ that will be held in_ _____.

(b)   Artist shall attend the dinner party prior to the aforementioned lecture.

2.   PAYMENT: In consideration of Company furnishing Artist's services hereunder, Purchaser shall pay to Company the sum of _____.

3.   TRANSPORTATION:
(a)   Purchaser agrees to pay for, at no cost to Artist or Company, two (2) round-trip first-class airline tickets for Artist and guest to be designated by Artist between Artist's residence and the place of contracted engagement.
(b)   Purchaser agrees to provide and pay for, at no cost to Artist or Company, (i) limousine transportation between Artist's residence and _____ airport upon departure and arrival, and (ii) limousine transportation between the local airport which Artist departs from and arrives at in connection with the_____.

4.   ACCOMMODATIONS/DRESSING ROOM:
(a)   Purchaser agrees to provide and pay for a suite at the_____.
(b)   Purchaser agrees to provide and pay for reasonable food and beverages for Artist.

5.   MISCELLANEOUS: This agreement constitutes the sole, complete and binding agreement between the parties hereto. This Agreement may not be changed, modified or altered except by an instrument in writing signed by the parties. This Agreement shall be construed in accordance with the laws of the State of California. Nothing in this Agreement shall require the commission of any act contrary to law or to any rule or regulation of any union, guild, or body having jurisdiction. Wherever or whenever there is any conflict between any provision of this Agreement and any such law, rule or regulation, then such law, rule or regulation shall prevail and this Agreement shall be curtailed, modified, or limited only to the extent necessary to eliminate such conflict.

6.   PARAGRAPH HEADINGS: The paragraph headings are inserted in this Agreement for convenience only and shall not be used in interpreting this Agreement.

IN WITNESS WHEREOF, the parties hereto have executed this Agreement on the date set forth below.

Date: _____
By: _____

BY:

Date: _____
By: _____

As an inducement to Purchaser to enter into the foregoing agreement, and as a material part of the consideration moving Purchaser to do so, I acknowledge that I have read the Agreement and I agree to be bound by its terms insofar as same apply to me.

Date: _____
By: _____

SAMPLE RIDER TO CELEBRITY CONTRACT

RIDER to the agreement dated _____, 19___ between _____ (hereinafter referred to as "Company") for the services of _____ (hereinafter referred to as "Artist") and _____ _____ (hereinafter referred to as "Purchaser").

It is mutually agreed between the parties as follows:

Purchaser hereby engages Company and Company hereby accepts such engagement hereinafter provided, upon all of the terms and conditions herein set forth.

To the extent any term or provision of this Rider conflicts with any term or provision of the agreement attached hereto, said term or provision of this Rider shall govern.

    1.   <u>ENGAGEMENT:</u>

(a)   The opening act, if any, for the engagement will be determined by Purchaser, subject to Company's approval, not to be unreasonably withheld, which opening act shall be the only act appearing with Artist.

(b)   One (1) hour shall be allocated to Artist's performance which, in Artist's sole discretion, shall be between forty-five (45) minutes and one (1) hour in length.

(c)   During Artist's performance and until Artist is completely offstage, there shall be no service permitted in the room in which Artist is performing and there shall be no delivery or collection of checks. Subject to the size and shape of the room, Artist in her sole discretion may consent to service at a reasonable periphery from the stage, but no service shall be permitted without Artist's prior written consent and no such service shall interrupt Artist's performance.

    2.   <u>REHEARSAL:</u> Purchaser shall provide with respect to Artist's performance, at its sole cost and expense, a sound and light rehearsal for one (1) hour, at a time to be mutually agreed upon by Purchaser and Artist. It is agreed that each such rehearsal shall be closed to all people except authorized personnel of Purchaser and guests of Artist.

    3.   <u>PAYMENT:</u> All deposit monies shall be paid as contracted hereunder, made payable to The _____ Company Client Trust Account, and sent to The _____ Company. Unless prior arrangements have been made, purchaser agrees to give to Artist's designee the balance of any monies due upon arrival in the city of performance, made payable to _____. No deductions may be made from Artist's check without prior written authorization. All other monies which are not payable during the engagement shall be made payable to The _____ Company.

    4.   <u>CANCELLATION CLAUSE:</u>

(a)   It is understood and agreed that Company shall have the right to cancel the engagement herein upon thirty (30) days' prior written notice to the Purchaser in the event that Artist's services are required in the preparation of, rehearsal or appearance in a motion picture; a Nevada, Atlantic City, New Jersey engagement; a free or pay television show and/or series; a commercial; or a legitimate stage production which would conflict with any part of the engagement hereunder.

(b)   Company's obligations in respect of the show are subject to Artist's detention or prevention by sickness, death, disability, inability to perform, accident, difficulties, epidemics, and any other cause, similar of dissimilar, beyond Artist's control. In the event of any such cancellation, deposit monies for the Show will be returned to Purchaser.

5.   INCIDENTALS TO PERFORMANCE:

(a)   Purchaser agrees to do and to furnish at its own expense all that is necessary for the proper presentation of Artist's performance and the rehearsals thereof, including, without limitation, suitable auditoriums (including without limitation a suitable stage), lighted, clean and in good order, public address systems in perfect working condition and the following incidentals:

(i)   Two (2) super trouper type follow spotlights, with operators;

(ii) Three (3) general lighting primary circuits (pink, red and blue);

(iii) Three (3) first-class microphones as follows:

(a) One (1) wireless microphone for Artist to use during her performance;

(b) One (1) offstage microphone with an "ON and OFF" switch, from which Artist's introduction will be made;

(c) One (1) "hardwired" microphone that will be used if there are any problems with the wireless microphone.

(iv) A technician familiar with each of the above microphones;

(v) A glass of water and Kleenex tissues to be placed in a convenient location near Artist during the rehearsals and during the performance.

(b)   In addition, Purchaser shall provide at its own expense, all stagehands, electricians, and any other labor as shall be necessary and/or required by any national or local union; all lights, tickets, house programs; all licenses (including musical performing rights licenses); ushers, ticket sellers and ticket takers; appropriate and sufficient advertising in the principal newspapers and Purchaser agrees to pay all necessary expenses in connection therewith. Purchaser agrees to pay all amusement taxes and to comply with all regulations and requirements of any national or local union that may have jurisdiction over any of the materials, facilities, services or personnel to be furnished by Purchaser, by Company or by Artist.

6.   ORCHESTRA: It is understood and agreed that Purchaser shall provide, at its sole cost and expense, a minimum backup of six (6) first-class musicians who read musical charts to play music before and/or during or immediately following Artist's performance. Instrumentation shall be piano, bass, drums, lead alto saxophone, trombone and trumpet. One member of said orchestra shall have a dual function as a musical conductor. If there are any additional musicians performing in connection with the engagement, or if there is a "house" orchestra, or if another Performer is using more musicians, then Artist reserves the right to utilize those musicians.

7.   BILLING: Artist shall receive one hundred percent (100%) sole star billing in any and all publicity releases and paid advertisements in connection with the engagement hereunder, including but not limited to programs, flyers, signs, lobby boards and marquees. No other name or photograph shall appear larger or more prominently than the credit and photograph of Artist, and no other name or photograph shall appear on the same line or above the name or photograph of Artist.

8.   PUBLICITY AND RIGHT TO SELL ITEMS:

(a)   Purchaser agrees to use only publicity material provided by Artist's Personal Manager and/or representative and further agrees that all advertising and publicity is subject to Company's approval prior to release.

(b)   Company shall have the right, but not the obligation, to sell souvenir programs and any other items related to Artist, including without limitation, phonograph records and videocassettes, in connection with and at the place of performance, and the receipts thereof shall belong exclusively to the Company.

9.   INTERVIEWS: Purchaser agrees not to commit Artist to any personal interviews or any other type of promotion or appearance without the prior consent of Artist or her representative. Purchaser

will not permit or authorize Artist's name to be used or associated with, directly or indirectly, any product or service without Artist's written consent. Purchaser will not permit or authorize the recording or broadcast, oral and/or visual, of any portion of performance without the express prior written consent of Artist or her representative.

10. DRESSING ROOM: Purchaser shall provide a first-class, private dressing room for Artist, at the place of performance, capable of being locked and with the best possible facilities available, including mirror, Kleenex tissues and towels, clothing rack with hangers, and electrical outlets. Purchaser agrees to ensure that within the confines of said dressing room Artist's privacy will be respected and that no one will be admitted other than individuals authorized by Artist.

11. TRANSPORTATION:

(a) Purchaser agrees to pay for, at no cost to Company, two (2) round-trip first-class non-stop airline tickets for Artist and one other person to be designated by Artist from Los Angeles, California to the place of contracted engagement. Reimbursement for this expense shall be at the time of signing of the agreement, made payable to the _____ Company and sent to _____ Company.

(b) Purchaser agrees to provide to Artist and one other person designated by Artist, at no cost to Company (i) exclusive (no person other than Artist and Artist's designee) first-class limousine transportation between the local airports which Artist departs from and arrives at in connection with the engagement and Artist's accommodations, (ii) exclusive (no person other than Artist and Artist's designee) first-class limousine transportation between the local airports which Artist departs from and arrives at in connection with the engagement and Artist's accommodations, (iii) exclusive (no person other than Artist and Artist's designee) first-class limousine transportation between Artist's accommodations and the place of the engagement.

12. ACCOMMODATIONS:

(a) Purchaser agrees to provide and pay for, at no cost to Artist or Company, a one-bedroom suite equipped with a refrigerator and one deluxe single room for each night of engagement.

(b) If travel arrangements necessitate, the accommodations will be available on the day before and the day after the engagement.

13. FOOD AND BEVERAGES: Purchaser agrees to provide and pay for, at no cost to Artist or Company, food and beverages consistent with Artist's stature and reputation, to Artist and Artist's traveling companion throughout the term of this engagement.

14. OBLIGATIONS: If before the date of the engagement it is found that Purchaser has not performed fully its obligations under any other agreement with any party for another engagement where it appears to Company in its sole determination that the financial credit of the Purchaser may be or has been impaired, Company may cancel this agreement and Purchaser shall forfeit any deposit monies. In the event that Purchaser does not perform fully all of its obligations herein, Company shall have the option to cause Artist to perform or refuse to perform hereunder and in either event, Purchaser shall be liable to Company for any cost, damage or expense (including attorneys' fees) incurred by Artist or Company as a result thereof, in addition to the compensation provided herein.

15. COMPANY'S REPRESENTATIVES AND WARRANTIES: Company represents and warrants that:

(a) it is a corporation, organized and validly existing under the laws of the state of its incorporation;

(b) it is free to enter into this Agreement and it has entered into an employment agreement with Artist pursuant to which Artist is obligated to render her services for Company and under said agreement with Artist, it has the right to control and lend Artist's services and grant the rights herein granted, and nether Company nor Artist is subject to any obligations or disability which will or might prevent or interfere with Company or Artist from fully keeping and performing all of the agreements, covenants and conditions to be kept or performed hereunder, and neither Company nor Artist has made nor will do, or omit to do, any act or thing which could or might interfere with or impair the complete enjoyment of the rights granted or the services to be rendered to Purchaser hereunder;

(c) it will perform all employer obligations in connection with Artist's services hereunder, including without limitation, the payment to Artist of all compensation or other consideration required to be paid under any agreement between Company and Artist and under any applicable collective bargaining agreement, and the payment of all union contributions and employer's share of withholding, employment or other taxes, which taxes are payable by reason of Artist's services hereunder.

16. <u>INDEMNITY</u>: Purchaser agrees to indemnify, defend and hold Company and Artist harmless from and against any and all losses, claims, damages, liabilities, demands, costs and expenses, including attorneys' fees, which may arise out of or derive from (I) the Show, and/or (ii) any breach or alleged breach by Purchaser of any representation, warranty, covenant or agreement made by Purchaser under this Agreement.

17. <u>ASSIGNMENT/JOINT VENTURE</u>: Purchaser shall not have the right to assign this Agreement or any provision hereof. Nothing herein contained shall ever be construed as to constitute the parties hereto as partners, or joint venturers, and neither Company nor Artist shall be liable in whole or in any part for any obligation that may be incurred by Purchaser in Purchaser's carrying out of any of the provisions hereof, or otherwise. The person executing this agreement on Purchaser's behalf warrants his/her authority to do so.

18. <u>PARAGRAPH HEADINGS</u>: The paragraph headings are inserted in this Agreement for convenience only and shall not be used in interpreting this Agreement.

IN WITNESS WHEREOF, the parties hereto have executed this Agreement on the date set forth below.

Date: _____
By: _____

Company: _____
Address: _____

Date: _____   By: _____

As an inducement to Purchaser to enter into the foregoing agreement, and as a material part of the consideration moving Purchaser to do so, I acknowledge that I have read the Agreement and I agree to be bound by its terms insofar as same apply to me.

Date: _____   By: _____

the star's booking. Celebrity Service lists the publicists, business managers (for legal and accounting matters), and agents that handle each star.

If a celebrity doesn't have a publicist but appears on a network television show, the show will have a publicist. Contact the television network and ask. The network publicist can usually put you in touch with the celebrity's personal manager, who is usually on call all the time. All the shows go on break for a period of the year. Find out when that is and see if the star might be available to travel then.

However, the personal manager is the toughest person to contact. Most rarely return calls to people they don't know. Persistence is often the key to getting through. Start calling well in advance, and always leave a message. You don't need to be rude. Politely let the person you speak with know you will continue to call until you reach the personal manager.

There is an organization of personal managers (see Chapter 12, Tools of the Trade) that maintains a membership list. Sometimes the celebrity's agent can supply it.

For almost any celebrity, you can contact their union, the Screen Actors Guild (SAG) or the American Federation of Television and Radio Actors (AFTRA) (see Chapter 12, Tools of the Trade). Both SAG and AFTRA have offices in New York or Los Angeles, and someone there can give you the name of the publicist or personal manager.

Once you find out what organization to call, make that call count. Persistence is more important than genius. It may take five or six (or more) calls to get through. As with personal managers, be polite. Just make it clear you will keep calling until you get to talk to someone who can give you an answer. Remember that publicists and managers may get as many as 500 calls a day, so you have only a minute or so to make your plea. Plan what you will say. (Perhaps even write out a script for yourself.) Make your pitch concise, and state clearly what's in it for the celebrity. If you have done your homework, mention why you know the person might want to help, and that they are in town (or nearby), the day you are planning the event.

An example: "I know Paul Newman will be in Miami for the Miami Grand Prix. I'd like him to attend a cocktail party. It's for the Burn Center, a cause I know he'd support, being a race car driver. I don't want him to perform. It will be positive publicity for him. The charity will provide transportation and security . . ."

Once you get a verbal commitment, follow it up with a formal letter of agreement, or ask for a written contract.

Thoroughly check the celebrity's standard contract, or have your lawyer do so. It should state that the celebrity is attending for free (or for whatever price you agree upon) and who is paying for extras (travel, room, and food, including what will be provided for those traveling with the star). Be specific. For example, if you don't plan to pay for long-distance phone calls, damaged hotel furniture, or room service, state this clearly in the written agreement, give a copy of the agreement to the hotel's front desk, and have the general manager sign it.

Do the same thing with limousine companies. Make it clear what the charity will be responsible for, and stipulate that the limo should get cash or credit cards from their customers. Some entertainers are infamous for taking advantage of charities this way.

Fundraisers unfamiliar with large-scale celebrity events can make very expensive mistakes. For example, a fundraiser new to such events cost his charity money by not dealing in writing with the management of a hotel at which a special event was held. A few weeks after the event, when the bills came in from the hotel, there was an additional bill from room service for $4,000 in champagne and caviar. The charges were made by the back-up singers of the entertainer who had performed at the event. The charity paid these unexpected expenses out of the money raised that evening, rather than harass the celebrity, who had given an excellent performance and helped attract a sell-out crowd.

> **TIP** Be sure that all hotel personnel — including the catering director, front desk manager, and general manager — are informed in writing as to what expenses the charity will pay.

If there are musicians involved, be sure you know what instruments you will have to provide and how many hours of rehearsal you must pay for. The rider should say that the entertainer is responsible for paying for any rehearsal overtime.

For newcomers to event production, spending the money to have an attorney review the agreement is invaluable. Or, ask a local concert promoter to be on your planning committee to provide advice for free or as part of his or her contribution.

Once you've lined up your star, you can reduce costs by getting things donated. Some hotels will provide free accommodations, and sometimes airlines will cover tickets. (Make sure these tickets are cancelable or can be changed, because they may need to be.) Sponsors love to have their pictures taken with celebrities. If possible, get the star's photo taken at the host hotel or with staff from your airline sponsor.

A travel agent can be a great committee person and can assist you in obtaining tickets and with complicated travel arrangements for celebrities and their entourages.

Like your mother, celebrities appreciate being met at the airport, staying at the locations they prefer, having rooms ready when they arrive, and having any special needs dealt with in advance. When Dick Clark and his wife, Kari, were to be in South America the week before the annual Bob Hope Gala of the National Parkinson Foundation in Miami, Kari asked if she could send their formal clothing in advance. The event manager picked it up. Since they were to arrive at 3 A.M., the Clarks planned to take a cab. But the event manager, who was familiar with the airport, knew he would have an easier time navigating than they would. He met the Clarks' flight, took them right to the limo, and on to the hotel, where he had already checked them in and hung their clothes in the closet. As a result, they were able to get some much-needed sleep before the event. Kari was so pleased she wrote the event manager a note of appreciation later.

If you handle business with a celebrity in a professional manner and establish a good rapport, you improve your chances of getting him or her to return in future years. Celebrities who are treated well may even lend their name to future mail campaigns and public service announcements. (If you want them to do this, make sure to discuss this in advance with their publicists.)

Remember that celebrities have lives of their own, too. Don't automatically assume that someone who has agreed to appear in a show will also attend a cocktail party or go to your house for din-

ner with you and your friends. If you want them to do that, ask beforehand and have it included in the contract. Some celebrities charge a fee for this. If the celebrity is unable to attend an additional function, ask if he or she will autograph some items that can be auctioned off or used as raffle prizes.

Even if you have taken every precaution and spelled out everything in the contract, something may go amiss. The University of Miami's Community Alliance Against AIDS discovered this when it staged "An Extraordinary Evening with Sophia Loren." This event, held on posh Williams Island, was a dinner under a tent for 600 people, and featured about 30 celebrities, including Julio Iglesias, Donna Summer, Petula Clark, and Donald O'Connor. Loren was the honoree.

In selling major donor tables (at $100,000 each), contributors were to have their photos taken with some of the celebrities. One couple wanted pictures taken with every star, especially Loren. After dinner, the event manager waded through Loren's fleet of bodyguards and explained that there was one couple with whom she needed to pose. She refused, saying she was still eating dinner. Later the couple was brought over to pose behind her while she remained seated, and she turned so her face wasn't visible. While the donors nevertheless made their sizable contribution to help the charity, part of their motivation had been the picture they had been promised, to which Loren had agreed. Fortunately, these particular donors were good sports. In general, it's wise to notify celebrities in writing that they will be expected to pose with donors.

While the previous example is extreme, remember when you are dealing with celebrities that their refusal to do something may not stem from a desire to be contrary, but because people routinely mob stars, grabbing at them and touching them. Understandably, some celebrities prefer to avoid this. Comedienne Joan Rivers, who stands a mere five feet tall, is always mobbed by her fans. But once she's committed to helping a worthy cause, there is no stopping her. When she appeared on stage in Miami after attending a crowded fundraising reception, she quipped, "For those of you who haven't touched me yet, I'll be back down there in a few minutes."

Chapter 9 Checklist

❑ Make a realistic entertainment budget. Be sure to include all incidentals.

❑ What type of celebrity can you afford?

❑ Watch television and check tabloids and trade magazines to see which celebrities support or have an interest in which charities.

❑ Check with area performance centers to see who is scheduled to appear around the date of your event.

❑ Schedule your event around the celebrity's itinerary.

❑ Plan your strategy for inviting the celebrity. If you know him or her, make personal contact. If not, locate the celebrity's publicist.

❑ Make a brief, businesslike proposal.

❑ Follow up the verbal commitment with a written contract or letter of agreement that clearly details what services you will and will not provide.

❑ Check the celebrity's standard contract requirements carefully (musicians, light, sound, staging, travel, entourage, etc.).

❑ Have an attorney or concert promoter review the contract.

❑ Seek donated services from hotels, airlines, limousine services, etc.

❑ Look for individual and corporate underwriting.

You have somehow survived the months of planning, dealing with personalities, and attending to the sea of details. Now the event is almost here. For the ultra-organized, little remains to be done. But in most cases, particularly for a seated event, staff members usually work right down to the wire. At some point, you have to say, "This is all we can do and this is how it will be." Say this *before* you stay up the whole night before. You will need energy for the big day.

chapter **10**

THE FINAL COUNTDOWN

Check and Recheck

If you have faithfully followed the instructions in this book, you now have a nice fat loose-leaf notebook. You have used the checklists to make sure everything has been covered. Now is the time to recheck. Go through each chapter checklist again. Having done that, you can be reasonably well assured that nothing has been forgotten. The day before the event, remind your support staff to be at the site at a specific time (well before the event's starting time) the next day.

Check with all the vendors to make sure they plan to show up on time. Get the phone numbers at which you can reach them outside of business hours. Check with each committee chairperson to make sure you know how to reach them if they won't be at their

Committee for the Breitman Institute of Science
1996 Annual Gala
at
Hotel InterContinental

Sunday, April 28, 1996

MINUTE BY MINUTE

9:00 a.m.   Stage set up (must be completed by 10:00 a.m. for AV set up)

10:00 a.m.   Set up by florist of party decor and flowers/Ballroom & Terrace

10:00 a.m.   Set up of registration tables, photo area, and information table on
              Terrace completed

10:00 a.m.   Begin sound and lights set up (Goldberg AV)

10:00 a.m.   Small stage and sound set up for musical trio on Terrace

12:00 p.m.   Tables and chairs set up in Ballroom & Terrace
              Dance floor installed in Ballroom

4:00 p.m.   Distribution of program books and favors on tables in Ballroom

5:15 p.m.   Valet opens

5:30 p.m.   Registration Table Opens
              Hosts and Hostesses in place

5:45 p.m.   Bars are open, cocktail reception begins with food service on
              Terrace

5:45-6:30 p.m. Musical trio begins playing

6:30 p.m.   Musical trio stops / complete orchestra in place in main Ballroom

6:45 p.m.   Orchestra plays opening dance set for 15 minutes

7:00 p.m.   RUSSELL SIMPSON welcomes guests

7:02 p.m.   MARVIN DUNCAN - Greetings

7:05 p.m.   RABBI IRA LEHMAN - Invocation

CANTOR STUART TUCHMAN - Israeli National Anthem
                            & Star Spangled Banner

7:10 p.m.   MARVIN DUNCAN returns
Presentations to Norma and Louis Stein & Herb Lowenthal
Acknowledgments

7:18 p.m.   STEPHEN KLEIN - Presentation of "Ambassadors for Breitman"

7:20 p.m.   MARVIN DUNCAN returns/DAVID ROSENTHAL gives gift to
Marvin

7:21 p.m.   DAVID ROSENTHAL - Keynote speaker

7:24 p.m.   Audiovisual Presentation - "The Future is in Our Hands"

7:29 p.m.   MARVIN DUNCAN comes to stage - Tribute to Simon Buchman II
                    1.) Read letter from President of Israel
                    2.) Presentation of antiquity
                    3.) Present bouquets at table to Cathy Buchman (Wife) and to
                            Jane Buchman (Mother)

Marvin Duncan returns to seat at head table.

7:31 p.m.   SIMON BUCHMAN - Response

7:35 p.m.   Band Leader announces Dinner
(While dinner is being served - 10 minute dance set to segue to   quiet
music while guests are eating)

Dance set 10 minutes while desert is being served

Black out Ballroom

8:30 p.m.   Off stage introduction of Michelle Meyer

Dance set

Guests leave - "Goodnight"

usual number. Make sure they have spoken with everyone on their lists: the decorator, band, caterer, florist, etc. If you haven't done it already, compile a one-page directory of the key people you might need to reach.

> **TIP** Arrange for a few people (family members, trusted friends, or assistants) to be with you on the day of the event to handle unexpected problems. You can dispatch them to put out the smaller fires while you handle the larger tasks.

Last-Minute Needs

No matter what the event, there are items you almost always need at the last minute. Invariably, these things are never around unless you have had the foresight to bring them yourself. Pack everything up in advance. Here is what you should bring with you:

ADMINISTRATIVE
- Contact list with home and work telephone numbers.
- Loose-leaf notebook with all contracts, contacts, etc. (plus some extra paper with holes already punched in)
- Payment for entertainer

AUDIOVISUAL
- Laptop computer and backup disks
- Black electrical tape/silver reflective tape
- Audio and video cassettes
- Extension cords—industrial strength and length
- Three-prong converter
- Flashlights
- Needle and thread
- Safety pins
- Walkie-talkies (or mobile phones or beepers)

PAPER PRODUCTS, OFFICE SUPPLIES, AND RELATED ITEMS
- Facial tissues
- Toilet tissue
- Paper towels
- Soap
- Trash bags
- Paper

- Scissors
- Signs
- Staple gun
- Masking and transparent tape
- Felt-tip waterproof markers (various sizes and colors)
- Paper clips
- Self-stick labels (various sizes)
- Poster board

FIRST-AID KIT
- Bandages
- Adhesive tape
- Stretch and gauze bandages
- Scissors/knife
- Tweezers
- Aspirin
- Antacid
- Alcohol and/or peroxide for disinfectant
- Sunscreen
- Insect repellent

STAFF FOOD
- Coffee
- Cold drinks
- Ice/ice chest
- Munchies

Pack up everything the day before the event, including the clothes you plan to wear. Then, on the day itself, all you have to do is pick up the box or suitcase in which you've packed things, and head out the door.

If the event is in a hotel, arrange to check in a day or two in advance so you can unpack, familiarize yourself with the place, and let everyone know where to reach you. Let the front desk staff know that you will be receiving a number of calls and tell them where you will be. If you have a beeper, leave that number with them. With all those things attended to, get a good night's sleep.

Registration

Registration sets the tone for the event because it is the first impression your group makes on those attending. If they have to wait in long lines, or if they're treated rudely or encounter problems, guests may be turned off before they get in the door. To prevent such problems, place only your brightest, most courteous, flexible people at the registration tables. However, you should emphasize that the main job of the registration staff is to sign in those attending, and make sure guests have paid and know where to go next.

Usually, the registration process is set up about three hours before the event. Even if your ballroom is not ready, your registration tables should be. They should be the first things that are functioning, since they are your guests' first stop.

There should be enough eight-foot-long tables to allow people to spread out a bit. Use long tables, covered attractively, with highly visible signs posted above them. You may need to use several tables, dividing them alphabetically, with each table handling a third or a fourth of the alphabet. Keep another table as a troubleshooting area, and one for VIPs. Place three or four chairs behind each table for registration personnel, even though they will probably wind up standing as guests file by.

> **TIP** Don't put signs on the tables themselves, because they will be covered up as people gather.

Make sure additional signs clearly point the way from the parking lot to the tables. Make sure there are enough lights and electrical outlets.

It is always better to have too many registration workers than too few. Use your judgment: For a gathering of 100 people, you might need only one registration worker per table. For 500 people, you may need four workers per table.

If you have to feed registration workers, do that first, then give them a chance to get dressed. And make sure everyone on the registration staff knows how to dress for the event. Usually, they wear the same type of apparel as those who attend the event.

If you are using computers, make sure they are all hooked up, functioning and in a secure area.

If the event is something more complicated or large-scale (for example, a tournament, -a-thon, or fair), you may need a separate set of registration tables for supervisors, referees, athletes, vendors, and sponsors. It is best to separate their check-in from that of the spectators, since they have different needs and may be arriving at different times.

You may need to give them their own registration forms, gifts, and information packets.

If this is an event with fixed seating, everyone should be given something with the number of his or her seat on it. It's a good idea to give out a slip of paper big enough not to be easily misplaced, but small enough to fit in a jacket pocket or small purse.

If you are concerned that there might be party crashers, distribute stickers, pins, or disposable bracelets to your guests to identify them.

At some events, the registration staff must collect money. Make sure they are equipped to do this, that they have a secure place to keep the money as well as calculators or adding machines and lists of those who have not paid.

To make payments easier for guests, consider arranging to take credit cards at the registration tables. Have a phone connected to the credit-card companies for immediate authorization.

Registration should never take more than an hour. If you have enough volunteers, each armed with a guest list, this is possible. All registration staff should be supplied with a list of everyone who is attending, listed both alphabetically and by table. This is also necessary because people don't want to wait in line for more than a few minutes.

> **TIP** Besides having sufficient staff at the registration desk, have additional greeters near the registration tables and posted in the main room to guide people to the proper spots.

No matter how good a job your committee does in arranging seating, there should be a troubleshooter to handle the last-minute changes that inevitably crop up. When this happens, a registration worker should immediately direct the person to the troubleshooter, who will make sure the problem is resolved. This way, everyone isn't delayed.

As with other aspects of the event, try to anticipate problems that might arise. If you use computers, make sure you have printed backup lists in case the computers conk out. If there is a problem with

> **TIP** Assigned seating isn't always necessary or desirable. At an auction or informal affair, let guests seat themselves. Registration for open seating takes much less time.

a guest's registration, be sure the workers know to smile at all times. They should apologize to guests for the problem and escort them to the troubleshooter's table, where someone will work with them until the problem is resolved. If the event is lengthy, try to arrange shifts for registration workers. Don't leave someone on duty for more than an hour or two at a time, because registration is a tiring job. Try to reward registration workers by giving them a good table at the event. Give them their meal free (if you can afford to), or at least make sure they get to see the show without charge.

Chapter 10 Checklist

❑ The day before the event, check with key committee chairpersons and vendors to make sure they know when to arrive.

❑ Compile a list of key contacts and their phone numbers in case a vendor fails to show or some other problem arises.

❑ Pack everything you will need the day before.

❑ Review your list of things to take and make sure everything is packed and can be found easily.

❑ If the event is at a hotel, check in a day ahead to set up a temporary control room.

❑ Those who will be working throughout the event should be given a meal, then allowed to change into proper attire before guests arrive.

❑ Set up the registration area.

❑ Make sure all computers at the registration tables are working.

❑ Check to make sure that all greeters are in the best location to help move the crowd along.

chapter 11

AFTER WORDS

Whether your event was a great success or much less than you'd hoped for, conducting a thorough review and critique can turn up valuable information that will be helpful when it comes time again to choose and plan another event.

Once everyone has recovered from the just-held event—at least a week but no more than a month afterwards—gather the key committee people together along with staff and pivotal volunteers to celebrate the event's conclusion. When you invite them, let everyone know there will be a brief review of the event to assess how things went and determine what could be improved upon should you hold the event again.

As a token of appreciation for everyone's hard work, have the gathering over lunch, either at a quiet restaurant or catered at someone's home. The charity should pay for this or find a source to underwrite it. Presenting small gifts to each of the participants is a nice touch, too.

The following post-event evaluation form is an easy format you can use for your event critique meeting. This form can be customized to include special aspects of your event or particular staffing issues. Make enough copies of the critique form so everyone who attends the meeting has one and you have enough left over for note taking and finally making a master form. Leave enough space between items so there is room for each person to write notes and personal observations as they review headings and questions prior to the discussion portion of the meeting.

Some organizations send the evaluation worksheet out in advance so those attending have time to think about it.

There should be a group leader or facilitator for the discussion. Choose either a well-liked volunteer, the special event coordinator or the executive director. Whoever runs it should emphasize that this is meant to be a time for *constructive* criticism. It should be a relaxed meeting where everyone feels comfortable participating.

Start off by thanking everyone again for their hard work. Clearly explain that this is a review process to improve future events, not a time to critique the participation of specific individuals. Go through every item in each section and seek input on those items that went awry, ways to improve things the next time.

 TIP This is also a choice time to enlist committee members and volunteers for a future event.

Afterwards, summarize the comments from the session, and have them typed and distributed, along with a thank-you note, to everyone who participated. Make a copy for your office event file or event notebook. This becomes your working paper for the next event.

Distribute a humorous hand-out such as this at a post-event evaluation meeting to add some levity and disperse any residual tensions.

6 PHASES OF A PROJECT

1. Enthusiasm
2. Disillusionment
3. Panic
4. Search for the Guilty
5. Punishment for the Innocent
6. Praise and Honors for the Non-participants

POST-EVENT EVALUATION

EVENT

- Was the event a good choice?

- Did people enjoy themselves?

- Did it attract the audience you targeted? If not, why?

- What could be changed to improve it?

- Did it conflict with another big event?

- Should it be held during the day instead of at night, or vice versa?

- Was it a fundraising or friend-raising event?

- How many people attended? Was that enough to make it worthwhile?

- Are more likely to attend the next time?

- Did it achieve the fundraising goal?

- Did it attract new donors and/or potential new donors?

- Did participants move into and up the donor pyramid?

- Did it need a rain date?

- Did the date set afford enough time to organize and promote the event?

- Was the event held at the optimum time of year?

COMMITTEES

- Did they complete assignments?

- Were tasks done in a timely manner and within budget?

- Did the chairpeople communicate regularly with the events manager?

- Did committee members ask for guidance/ assistance when needed?

- Were there enough/too many people on each committee?

- Did the committees meet regularly enough/ too often?

- Have any new leaders emerged from within the committees?

LOCATION

- Was the site the best one for the event?

- Did the site accommodate the number of people you were expecting?

- Might you need a larger or smaller site the next time?

- Was weather a consideration?

- Was the site's available equipment adequate (enough tables, chairs, staging, kitchen facilities)?

- If you used rentals, was the equipment in good condition?

- How do you rate the rental company?

- Could this event have been held at a less expensive/complicated site?

- Was the site convenient for those attending?

- Was there access to public transportation?

- Was the facility accessible to the physically challenged?

- Was there adequate parking at a reasonable price?

- Were special permits/insurance required? Was this very expensive?

- Did you consider weather insurance (for an outdoor event)?

BUDGET

- Did you stay within your guidelines?

- How much did the event cost? How much did it make? (Percentage ratio?)

- Were there particular budget line items that significantly exceeded estimates?

- Was the amount you spent consistent with your organization's image and goals?

- Did the amount you raised warrant such an event?

- Did you have enough front money? Adequate cash flow?

- Was the bookkeeping done throughout the event development to monitor expenses?

- Did your bookkeeping system adequately track all expenses and income?

- Were all bills paid on time?

- Were contracts negotiated so as to maximize fundraising?

- Did you explore all possibilities for under-writing and sponsorships?

- Were there items missing from the budget? List them.

- If you were to do this again, how could you cut expenses and maximize income?

- Were there any financial surprises?

PUBLICITY

- Did you have enough lead time to obtain the publicity you needed?

- Did you get news releases to the right sources?

- Was your media list adequate?

- How could you have attracted more publicity?

- If publicity was handled by a staff person, did he/she need more help?

- If handled by volunteers, would they have benefited from some professional guidance/help?

- Did you stay within your budget?

- Were mailings sent out in a timely manner?

- Did you contact all community calendars available?

- Did you make the most of local media including cable access stations?

- Did you make use of electronic media, including e-mail and a web page?

- Was there adequate follow-up and coordination?

- Were the invitations/flyers/posters attractive?

- Was distribution good?

- Were the mailing lists up to date? Did you receive a large number of returns?

REGISTRATION

- Did registration go smoothly?

- Was the registration table easy to find?

- Were there enough registration staff members on duty to prevent long lines?

- Any major problems? Complaints from guests?

- Were volunteers properly trained?

- Was registration staff properly dressed and courteous?

- Did you use computers? Was there a backup system?

- If you used computers, did they function properly?

FOOD

- Was the food good? bad? a little of both?

- Did you hold a food tasting prior to the event?

- Were there any complaints about the meal or the service?

- How was the presentation?

- If your group cooked or brought food, were there any problems?

- Were there enough volunteers and staff for set-up and clean-up?

- Did you stay within the budget?

- Could it have been less expensive if you hired someone else or used a different location?

- Were you able to accommodate special dietary restrictions?

- Was the beverage and liquor service adequate? What would you change?

- Did you attempt to get food, beverages, and/or liquor donated or underwritten?

ENTERTAINMENT

- Did it enhance the event?

- Was it appropriate to the theme?

- Was it within the budget?

- Did people dance (if there was a band/DJ) or enjoy the show?

- Were the sound and light systems adequate and functioning properly?

- Did you hire a firm to handle all A/V requirements?

- Were you satisfied with the firm's performance?

- Could better entertainment have been obtained at the same price or less?

- Were contracts properly negotiated and reviewed?

- Did you take advantage of the publicity potential of well-known entertainers?

- Did you request the celebrity create publi service announcements for your organization?

- Did you explore getting celebrity's transportation, lodging, and related costs sponsored?

- Could the event still have been successful without entertainment/celebrity participation?

EVENT MANAGEMENT

- Was your manager able to handle all aspects of the event professionally?

- Did the manager make all assignments clear and follow up on committee members' progress?

- Did the manager handle contract negotiations? Attempt to lower costs where possible?

- Was there proper staff available to assist the manager?

- How did the manager relate to regular staff and volunteers?

- Was the manager readily available when problems arose?

- Were there any emergencies, personality problems, or serious logistical mistakes?

- Was the manager a staff person or consultant?

chapter 12

TOOLS OF THE TRADE

Now that you know how to create a great special event, here are some expert sources and resources that can help you make it even better.

Fundraising and Trade Organizations

AMERICAN ASSOCIATION OF FUNDRAISING
COUNSEL
25 W 43rd St., Suite 820
New York, NY 10036
Phone: (212) 354-5799
Fax: (212) 768-1795

Professional organization of fundraising consulting firms. Publishes *Giving USA,* an annual guide that contains national statistics on fundraising and fundraising trends.

AMERICAN MANAGEMENT ASSOCIATION
135 W 50th St.
New York, NY 10020
Phone: (212) 586-8100
Fax: (212) 903-8168
The American Management Association is a trade group for management professionals. The AMA runs a subsidiary called Trainers Workshop, through which is available its monthly publication, *Trainers Workshop*. Each issue focuses on an aspect of management. It comes with lecture materials, group exercises and handouts you can use to run your own training session. To order: Trainers Workshop, P.O. Box 319, Trudeau Road, Saranac Lake, N.Y. 12983. Phone (518) 891-1500. FAX (518) 891-0368.

ASSOCIATION FOR HEALTH CARE PHILANTHROPY
313 Park Ave., Suite 400
Falls Church, VA 22046
Phone: (703) 532-6243
Fax: (703) 532-7170
A professional group offering education and networking for health-care professionals.

BUSINESS COMMITTEE FOR THE ARTS, INC.
1775 Broadway, Suite 510
New York, NY 10019
Phone: (212) 664-0600
Fax: (212) 956-5980
Encourages businesses to support the arts. Offers many publications and a quarterly newsletter.

COMMUNITY CONCERTS
111 W 57th St., Suite 418
New York, NY 10019-2276
Phone: (212) 307-4000
Fax: (212) 333-3117
A nonprofit organization located in 600 cities in the United States and Canada. It helps community groups book and promote musical events, including fundraisers.

COUNCIL FOR ADVANCEMENT & SUPPORT OF EDUCATION (CASE)
11 Dupont Circle, Suite 400
Washington, DC 20036
Phone: (202) 328-5936 or 5996
Fax: (202) 387-4973

An organization geared mainly toward colleges and private schools. It publishes *CASE Currents*, a magazine that offers ideas for special events. Also publishes various books and runs seminars in various locales and at various levels, for beginners through seasoned professionals.

COUNCIL OF BETTER BUSINESS BUREAUS PHILANTHROPIC ADVISORY SERVICE
4200 Wilson Blvd.
Arlington, VA 22203
Phone: (703) 276-0100
Fax: (703) 525-8277
A national clearinghouse of information on non-profit organizations. Sets standards for nonprofit organizations. Offers many publications, reports on charities.

INDEPENDENT SECTOR
1828 L St. NW
Washington, DC 20036
Phone: (202) 223-8100
Fax: (202) 467-0609
Nonprofit coalition that encourages charitable giving and volunteerism. Offers many publications.

INTERNATIONAL ASSOCIATION OF FAIRS AND EXPOSITIONS
3043 East Cairo
P.O. Box 985
Springfield, MO 65801
Phone: (417) 862-5771
Fax: (417) 862-0156
Provides management of fairs and expositions, offers many catalogs and services. It compiles lists of major fairs and expositions throughout the United States and in various parts of the world. Fundraisers might use this to find out about events in their area, then seek to tie a fundraiser to them. The group's magazine also includes listings of goods, services, supplies, and entertainment suppliers.

MEETING PROFESSIONALS INTERNATIONAL
1950 Stemmons Freeway
Dallas, TX 75207-3109
Phone: (214) 712-7700
Fax: (214) 712-7770
Professional educational society that serves as a

resource for businesses and meeting professionals. It has a resource center that offers information on how to organize meetings and conventions.

NATIONAL ASSOCIATION OF CATERING
EXECUTIVES
60 Revere Dr., Suite 500
Northbrook, IL 60662
Phone: (847) 480-9080
Fax: (847) 480-9282
This trade group for food professionals operates a certification program for catering executives and will refer inquiries to certified association members in cities throughout the country.

NATIONAL CATHOLIC DEVELOPMENT
CONFERENCE
86 Front St.
Hempstead, NY 11550
Phone: (516) 481-6000
Fax: (516) 489-9287
The major association of Catholic fundraising organizations, publishing many periodicals, including *Fund Raising Forum*.

NATIONAL SOCIETY OF FUND RAISING
EXECUTIVES (NSFRE)
1101 King St., Suite 700
Alexandria, VA 22314
Phone: (703) 684-0410
Fax: (703) 684-0540
Provides guidance and assistance to fundraising professionals. Publishes a quarterly journal and a newsletter and provides an executive search service.

NATIONAL SPEAKERS ASSOCIATION
1500 S. Priest Drive
Tempe, AZ 85281
Phone: (602) 968-2552
Fax: (602) 968-0911
This group educates professional speakers.

PROFESSIONAL CONVENTION MANAGEMENT
ASSOCIATION
100 Vestavia Parkway, Suite 220
Birmingham, AL 35216
Phone: (205) 823-7262
Fax: (205) 822-3891
Publishes bimonthly magazine, *Convene*, which discusses ethics, public speakers, and other topics

primarily for convention managers but could be helpful to nonprofit groups.

PUBLIC RELATIONS SOCIETY OF AMERICA
33 Irving Place, Third Floor
New York, NY 10003
Phone: (212) 995-2230
Fax: (212) 995-0757
The world's largest organization for public relations professionals offers a variety of professional development resources including the quarterly magazine, *Public Relations Strategist*, monthly newspaper, *Public Relations Tactics*, a job newsletter, seminars, and national conferences. Subscriptions are $25 for members, $40 for non-members.

SOCIETY FOR NONPROFIT ORGANIZATIONS
6314 Odana Rd., Suite 1
Madison, WS 53719
Phone: (608) 274-9777
Fax: (608) 274-9978
Offers a variety of books and periodicals to help nonprofit groups.

TOASTMASTERS INTERNATIONAL
23182 Arroyo Vista
Rancho Santa Margarita, CA 92688
Phone: (714) 858-8255
Fax: (714) 858-1207
Trains speakers for nonprofit education leadership and communications. Offers many publications.

Fundraising Publishers

AMERICAN COUNCIL FOR THE ARTS
1 East 53rd St.
New York, NY 10022
Phone: (212) 223-2787
Fax: (212) 223-4415
Publishes an association newsletter and a number of journals. Runs clearinghouse with information on arts policy, management, and education programming.

AMERICAN HOSPITAL PUBLISHING
737 N. Michigan Ave., Suite 700
Chicago, IL 60611
Phone: (312) 951-1100
Fax: (312) 951-8491
Publishes materials for hospital management pro-

fessionals, including *The Volunteer Leader*, a monthly publication that focuses on how to administer hospital-related volunteer programs, dealing with volunteers and organizing events.

CHRONICLE OF PHILANTHROPY
1255 23rd St. NW
Washington, DC 20037
Phone: (202) 466-1200
Fax: (202) 296-2691
A biweekly newspaper for the nonprofit world. It includes news and information on fundraisers. Almost every issue has a column about special events. An index of previously published articles is available.

THE FOUNDATION CENTER
79 5th Ave.
New York, NY 10003
Phone: (212) 620-4230
Fax: (212) 691-1828
Offers publications, seminars, a reference library.

HOKE COMMUNICATIONS, INC.
224 7th St.
Garden City, NY 11530-5771
Phone: (516) 746-6700 or (800) 229-6700
Fax: (516) 294-8141
Publishes direct marketing and fundraising monthly newsletters. It has an extensive library of printed and video reference materials.

INTERNATIONAL EVENTS GROUP (IEG)
640 N. LaSalle, Suite 600
Chicago, IL 60610
Phone: (312) 944-1727
Fax: (312) 944-1897
Compiles a variety of resources invaluable to fundraisers. One is a computer disk that lists 1,800 top national sponsors and which ones prefer what sorts of events. This comes in the form of a revolving card index, too. It offers listings on which sponsors prefer golf, opera, or food events and the most active sponsors in your market. Another index lists categories (financial services, transportation, etc.) and sponsors who offer them. There is also a newsletter that profiles sponsors and examines how they decide which charities to support.

NEW YORK PUBLICITY OUTLETS
Public Relations Plus Inc.
P.O. Box 1197
New Milford, CT 06776
Phone: (800) 999-8448
Cost: $185 per year
The semi-annual guide to who does what in broadcasting and print in New York City. This 40-year-old veteran publication contains listings for about 4,000 media outlets and 10,000 key media contacts at newspapers, magazines, broadcast and cable TV networks, radio, news services, African-American and ethnic publications. Listings include names, addresses, titles, beats, e-mail, direct-dial telephones, and fax numbers.

metro CALIFORNIA media
Phone: (800) 999-8448
Public Relations Plus, Inc.
(See address above)
Cost: $185 per year
What *New York Publicity Outlets* is to the Big Apple, this guide is for print and broadcasting for the whole state of California. Published semiannually for 20 years, it lists 4,000 media outlets and 10,000 key media contacts. See above for details.

SPECIAL EVENTS MAGAZINE
Miramar Communications, Inc.
23815 Stuart Ranch Road
Malibu, CA 90265
Phone: (800) 543-4116 or (310) 317-4522
Fax: (310) 317-9644
A monthly magazine that also publishes an annual product and source guide.

Celebrity Special Events Resource List

ARTIST SERVICES, INC.
1017 O Street NW
Washington, DC 20001
Phone: (202) 265-4100
Fax: (202) 265-4161
E-mail address: cyoe.asi@cpo.com
This firm books artists to perform at nonprofit fundraising and special events. It specializes in producing multi-artist combinations for an event. ASI also handles tour management of stars such as Marvin Hamlisch, Maureen McGovern, and others.

BILLBOARD'S INTERNATIONAL TALENT &
TOURING DIRECTORY
1515 Broadway
New York, NY 10036-8986
Phone: (212) 764-7300
Fax: (212) 536-5358

CARDIFF PUBLISHING CO.
P.O. Box 900189
San Diego, CA 92120
Phone: (619) 286-6902
Publishes the *Big Celebrity Address Book*, containing some 20,000 addresses for $44.70.

COLLECTOR'S BOOK STORE
1708 N. Vine St.
Hollywood, CA 90028
Phone: (213) 467-3296

CELEBRITY SERVICES INTERNATIONAL INC.
Mark Kerrigan
Celebrity Service Intl., Inc.
1780 Broadway, Suite 300
New York, NY 10019
Phone: (212) 245-1460
or
Jeff Kormos
Celebrity Service Intl., Inc.
8833 Sunset Blvd., Suite 401
Los Angeles, CA 90069
Phone: (310) 652-1700

A databank of more than 500,000 names of celebrities and newsmakers. Five major services provided only to subscribers include:

Daily Bulletin: a daily tracking of the whereabouts of celebrities, including how to make contact.

Telephone Service: a daily phone service to gain instant information on major personalities.

International Social Calendar: a listing of international social events for partygoers, charities, social planners, and jet setters.

Theatrical calendar: a compilation of theatrical activities, including openings, productions, and casting opportunities.

Special services: handles activities related to openings and new products, including the appearances of celebrities at business, charity, and fundraising events.

Contact book: a concise, comprehensive directory of the top personalities and organizations dealing with the entertainment industry for eight cities: New York, San Francisco, Hollywood, Washington, Toronto, London, Paris, and Rome.

VARIETY
(Weekly and daily)
249 W. 17th St., 4th floor
New York, NY 10011
Phone: Sales and advertising: (212) 337-7002
          Subscriptions: (800) 323-4345
Fax: (212) 337-6975
The trade magazine for the entertainment field.

Celebrity Sources

AMERICAN FEDERATION TELEVISION AND RADIO ARTISTS (AFTRA)
6922 Hollywood Blvd., 8th Floor
Hollywood, CA 90028
Phone: (213) 461-8111
or
260 Madison Ave., 7th floor
New York, NY 10016
Phone: (212) 532-0800

AMERICAN SOCIETY OF COMPOSERS, AUTHORS AND PUBLISHERS (ASCAP)
1 Lincoln Plaza
New York, NY 10023
Phone: (212) 595-3050

AUTO CLERK SERVICES
1821 Glenwood Road
Glendale, CA 91201
Phone: (818) 550-7317
Fax: (818) 500-7319
Offers a listing for more than 11,000 home addresses for celebrities. The directory is updated a few times a year.

SCREEN ACTORS GUILD (SAG)
5757 Wilshire Blvd.
Los Angeles, CA 90036
Phone: (213) 954-1600
or
1515 Broadway
New York, NY 10036
Phone: (212) 944-1030

Full-Service Event Production Companies

ARTIST SERVICES, INC.
1017 O Street NW
Washington, DC 20001
Phone: (202) 265-4100
Fax: (202) 265-4161
Produces staged events for nonprofits with one or more music stars.

RADIO CITY MUSIC HALL PRODUCTIONS
1260 Avenue of the Americas
New York, NY 10020
Phone: (212) 246-4600
Large-scale international and national events, comprehensive planning and implementation. Creates one-time events as well as those with ongoing potential.

Speakers Bureaus

HARRY WALKER INC.
1 Penn Place
Suite 2400
New York, NY 10119
Phone: (212) 563-0700
The nation's foremost people, including former presidents, economists, media (Ted Koppel, Tom Brokaw and John Chancellor), newspaper columnists (Ann Landers), political figures and other individuals from the worlds of show business, religion, and sports, can be booked through this firm.

DMB SPEAKERS BUREAU
7800 Red Road
Miami, FL 33143
Phone: (305) 662-9190
Fax: (305) 662-9965
One of the nation's largest booking services, specializing in celebrities, sports, politics and literature.

GREATER TALENT NETWORK
150 5th Avenue
New York, NY 10011
Phone: (212) 645-2000
Fax: (212) 627-1471
Online: http://www.greatertalent.com

Can book a variety of celebrity speakers such as Kareem Abdul-Jahbar, Ben and Jerry, Michael Moore, and Olympia Dukakis. Check the web page for details.

Book References

Brentlinger, Marliyn E., and Judith M. Weiss, *The Ultimate Benefit Book: How to Raise $50,000 Plus for Your Organization*, Octavia Press, Cleveland, OH, 1987.

Brody, Ralph, and Marcia Goodman, *Fund-Raising Events: Strategies and Programs for Success*, Human Sciences Press, Cleveland, OH, 1988.

Czuckrey, William, *Games for Fundraising: How to construct and play hundreds of games to raise money for your organization*, Pineapple Press, Sarasota, FL, 1995.

Devney, Darcy Campion, *Organizing Special Events and Conferences: A Practical Guide for Busy Volunteers and Staff*, Pineapple Press, Sarasota, FL, 1990.

Dunn, Thomas G., *How to Shake the Money Tree: Creative Fund-Raising for Today's Nonprofit Organizations*, Viking Penguin, New York, 1988.

Drotning, Phillip T., *500 Ways for Small Charities to Raise Money*, Public Service Materials Center, Washington, D.C.

Gale Research, *501 Business Leads: The Ultimate Guide to Cutting through Red Tape and Making the Contacts You Need*, Citadel Press Group,. Carol Publishing Group, New York, 1994.

Geier, Ted, *Cause Effective*, Nonprofit Resource Development Center, New York, 1986.

Graham, Christine, *Keep the Money Coming: A Step-by-Step Guide to Annual Fundraising*, Pineapple Press, Sarasota, FL, 1992.

Graham, Stedman, Joe Jeff Goldblatt and Lisa Delpy, *The Ultimate Guide to Sport Event Management and Marketing*, Irwin Publishing, Burr Ridge, IL, 1995. Call (800) 634-3966.

Harris, April L., *Special Events: Planning for Success*, Council for Advancement and Support of Education, Washington, DC, 1988.

Kraatz, Katie and Julie Haynes, *The Fundraising Formula: 50 Creative Events Proven Successful Nationwide*, Fundraising Institute, A Division of The Taft Group, Gale Research, Detroit, MI, 1987.

Lagauskas, Valerie, *Parades: How to Plan, Promote and Stage Them*, Sterling Publishing Co., Inc., New York, 1982.

Lawrence, Elizabeth, *The Complete Caterer: A Practical Guide to the Craft and Business of Being a Caterer*, Doubleday, New York, 1988.

Miller, Donna, *A Guide to Catering: Catering Your Own Events or Hiring Professionals*, DJ's Guides, Portland, OR, 1986.

Ninkovich, Thomas, *The Reunion Handbook*, The National Reunion Association, Nevada City, CA, 1983.

O'Connell, Brian, *The Board Member's Book*, The Foundation Center, New York, 1985.

Pressner, Gerald M., *Golf Tournament Management Manual*, Non-Profit Network, Arcadia, CA, 1986.

Pressner, Gerald M., "Charity Auction Management Manual," Non-Profit Network, Arcadia, CA, 1986.

Reisfeld, Randi, *The Bar/Bat Mitzvah Survival Guide*, Citadel Press Book, Carol Publishing Group, New York, 1992.

Reynolds, Renny, *The Art of the Party*, Penguin Books, New York, 1992.

Sheerin, Mira, "How to Raise Top Dollars from Special Events," Public Service Materials Center, Hartsdale, NY, 1984.

Setterberg, Fred and Kary Schulman, *Beyond Profit: The Complete Guide to Managing the Nonprofit Organization*, Harper & Row Publishers Inc., New York, 1985.

Stewart, Martha, *Entertaining,* Clarkston and Potter, New York, 1982.

Computer Resources

CYBERSPACE PR REPORT
Public Relations Society of America
Subscription Department
33 Irving Place
New York, NY 10211
This is an interactive newsletter as well as a tutor geared to help public relations professionals use computers more effectively.

IMPACT ONLINE
Cindy Shove, Executive Director
Phone: (415) 327-1389
E-mail address: http://www.impactonline.org
Nonprofit organizations can create their own World Wide Web pages as part of a Web site maintained by the organization, Impact Online. Based in San Jose, Calif., the group has created an on-line application process for charities that want to reach potential donors and volunteers. The service is free.

Software Programs

A-THON TRACKER
Northwest Software Technologies
2418 California Ave., Suite A
Everett, WA 98201
Phone: (206) 252-7287
Fax: (206) 742-6719
Online: http://home.sprynet.com/sprynet/nsti
Price: $495 for single user, $995 for network.
This program is designed to help charities manage walk-a-thons, dance-a-thons and other events for which volunteers solicit sponsors to make contributions. It generates tax receipts for donors, guests, and sponsors.

AUCTION-TRACKER
Northwest Software Technologies
(see address, phone, and URL, above)
Price: $995 for single user; $1,895 for network.
This software helps manage charity fundraising auctions. Generates tax receipts for donors, guests, and sponsors.

BANQUET-TRACKER
Northwest Software Technologies
(see address, phone, and URL, above)
Price: $495 for single user, $995 for network.
This program is designed to help charities manage
fundraising banquets, can be used to track outright
gifts and pledges, send bills on cycle, and generate
tax receipts.

EVENT
RAISER'S EDGE FOR WINDOWS
Blackbaud
4401 Belle Oaks Drive
Charleston, SC 29405
Phone: (800) 443-9441
Software that provides profiles from previous
events, organizes and analyzes upcoming event
information, creates lists for registration, seating,
etc. It includes event income, expense and
summary reports.

THE EVENT MANAGER
Phoenix Solutions
39560 Stevenson Place, Suite 112
Freemont, CA 94539
Phone: (800) 914-5275
Fax: (510) 713-7559
Price: Starts at $2,450
This software helps charity officials manage special
fundraising events, creates time lines and budgets,
tracks ticket sales and pledge payments, plans seating assignments, prints name tags and thank-you
notes. Also transfers information into charity's
databases.